The Apostle Paul's
LETTERS
FROM
PRISON

Bennie Goodwin, Ph.D.

Editor

A UMI Publication

Publisher
Urban Ministries, Inc.
P. O. Box 436987
Chicago, Illinois 60643-6987

ISBN: 0-940955-24-5
Second Edition
Catalog No. 9-2798

Scripture quotations are from the King James Version of the Bible unless otherwise stated. Printed in the United States of America.

DEDICATION

This book is dedicated to the memory of Dr. Walter L. Banks, whose love and commitment to teaching the Scriptures have been a great inspiration to so many pastors and students of the Word of God.

CONTENTS

ACKNOWLEDGEMENTS 11

INTRODUCTION *Dr. Bennie Goodwin* 13

GALATIANS: A Letter of Defense
Professor Marvin Goodwin 15

EPHESIANS: A Letter of Encouragement
Dr. Mary Carr 27

PHILIPPIANS: A Letter of Joy
Dr. Bennie Goodwin 39

COLOSSIANS: A Letter of Christ's Superiority
Dr. Kenneth Hammonds 57

PHILEMON: A Letter of Love
Fred Thomas 71

Footnotes
Bibliography
Biographies

ACKNOWLEDGMENTS

We wish to acknowledge the outstanding contributions of publications manager and designer, Shawan Brand; copy editor, Mary C. Lewis; proofreader: Connie Taylor; (Cover design) Grant Hoekstra Graphics, Inc., and publications assistants, Carolyn Cummings, Caron B. Davis and Cheryl Wilson, without whose help this book could not have come into existence. Last but not least, we wish to thank Media Graphics Corporation and Dickinson Press, Inc.

INTRODUCTION

Dr. Bennie Goodwin

What do these five persons have in common—Martin Luther King, Jr., Mohandus Gandhi, John Bunyan, Malcolm X, and St. Paul? You're right, if you said that all of them had been to jail. You're right again if you said that they gave hope to the world because of their imprisonment.

It was while Malcolm X was in a prison near Boston, Massachusetts that he turned from a life of crime and debauchery to a career of religious leadership and social uplift. In prison Gandhi continued developing his philosophy of social change through non-violent passive resistance. It was in prison that John Bunyan wrote *Pilgrim's Progress*. Martin Luther King, Jr. wrote "Letter From A Birmingham Jail" and St. Paul wrote most of his 12 or 13 letters that are preserved in the New Testament.

To many of the Black men and women who comprise a disproportionately high percentage of the U.S. prison population, incarceration is a violent and terribly depressing place. But for the Apostle Paul it was a place to minister, preach, teach, and write.

We are grateful to the dedicated Christians who helped us write this book which focuses on some of Paul's most well-known letters (Galatians, Ephesians, Philippians, Colossians and Philemon.) Each letter is unique in its content and central message. But all of them have a foundation of faith in God through Jesus Christ, an aroma of love and the upward look of hope. Each letter conveys the attitude of a man who experienced a radical, positive change in spiritual direction and was determined to work in partnership with God and people to bring the Good News to the whole world. These letters were written by a man who had focused his complete attention on God through Jesus Christ. This man had one goal in life to please God and make Jesus Christ known. No wonder his letters and his work helped change the Roman empire and are still being used by God, almost 20 centuries later, to convict sinners and challenge saints to do God's will.

To read this book will help you, but, to receive a greater benefit from this book, we suggest these steps:

Step 1: Choose one of these letters, sit down and read it all the way through in one sitting, if possible, in the KJV (King James Version) or whatever version of translation with which you are most familiar.

Step 2: Go back and read the same letter in another version or translation, maybe the NIV (New International Version) or the TEV (Today's English Version) also known as Good News for Modern Man).

Step 3: Turn to the commentary on your chosen letter in this book. Read what the author has to say about the city and people to whom the letter is addressed; also notice the letter's structure, analysis and central message.

Step 4: Read the *Scripture Focus* verses and answer the *Scripture Search* questions near the end of the chapter.

Step 5: Go back and read the entire New Testament letter again in your favorite Bible and respond to the *African American Connection* section.

By the end of Step 5, the letter will probably have a new freshness to you. In addition to new knowledge and understanding, expect a new perspective that will make you eager to share your knowledge, feelings and enthusiasm with your students, family, friends and colleagues.

At the end of this book, there is a list of books for further reading and research.

It is our prayer, that this book will enrich your personal spiritual life and better equip you to share with others what you have learned. "The things that you have learned from me before many witnesses, pass on those same things to other dependable people, so that they can teach the same things to others." (2 Timothy 2:2, paraphrased).

GALATIANS:
A Letter of Defense

Professor Marvin Goodwin
Galatians 1:1-8; 2:20; 5:1-6

THE GALATIANS

The Galatians, like the inhabitants of the surrounding country, worshiped the mother of gods, named Agdistis.

The possessors of Galatia were of three different nations or tribes of Gauls: the Tolistologi, the Trocmi, and the Tectosagi. The term "Galatia" does not describe a single city or state. The name was first used for an area in the central plateau region of Asia Minor inhabited from 275 B.C., by a people known as "Galatians." After the death of its king, Amyntas in 25 B.C., the kingdom of Galatia—with its chief cities of Ancyra, Tavium, and Pessinus—was incorporated into a Roman province carrying the name of its older territory. This Galatian district was situated in the highlands, several thousand feet above sea level. This new province was extended to include the cities of Inconium, Lystra, Derbe and Pisidian Antioch. At the time when Paul and others "preached out" (founded) the churches of Galatia, the province had been extended to include the territories of Paphlagonia and Pontus. Thus, in Paul's letter to the Galatians, he addresses the churches located throughout the whole of the north-central region of Asia Minor, containing some 14 cities in all, of which Iconium was the most celebrated.[1]

It is possible that while Peter was making converts in one part of Galatia, the Apostle Paul was in another. Claiming authority from Peter, some converts expressed views that contrasted with Paul's; to expose and correct these differences was one intention of this epistle.[2]

THE LETTER

Character and Significance

In the Book of Galatians, as in Romans, we meet many of the weightiest themes of Paul's preaching: justification by faith, life in Christ, the responsibilities of love, the meaning of the Cross, the function of Mosaic Law, and life in the Spirit. In Galatians however, Paul is not as free to develop and comment on these ideas in his own way as he is in Romans. He is caught up in the heat of controversy—as the frequently broken syntax of his sentences indicates. He had to defend not only the chief points of his Gospel message but also his apostolic credentials.

In the Galatian letter, Paul is in a battle for the hearts and minds of the Galatian church community. If he loses his fight, Christianity for the Galatians might have merely become another radical Jewish sect, and nothing more. If Paul had failed in his battle, thousands upon thousands of today's Christian community might not have ever come to the knowledge of Christ our Saviour.[3] Therefore, this letter is written with great vigor and feeling. Although it is at times somewhat erratic, its argument is often hard to follow, its tone frequently harsh, its meaning sometimes obscure, and its substantive issues sometimes overshadowed by personal feeling. Yet precisely because Paul here throws himself without reserve into the proclamation of the Gospel, the letter has a power unique among his writings and has exerted an influence out of all proportion to its modest length.[4]

MAIN THEMES

Galatians' main themes are: 1) a defense of the doctrine of justification by faith; 2) warnings against regression to Judaism and 3) a vindication of Paul's apostleship.

16

Key Verse

"I am astonished that you are so quickly deserting the one who called you by the grace of Christ and are turning to a different gospel" (1:6, NIV).

The Galatian Christians had been brought to Christ by the ardent and powerful preaching of the Apostle Paul. It appears that these brethren had been saved for two or three years, and that in Paul's absence they had been tempted into a change of allegiance by the Judaizers who sought to convert them from the teaching of Paul's Gospel. Therefore Paul expresses, in the mildest manner possible, his astonishment at their defection. Paul was deeply affected and amazed that such a thing could have happened.[5] They had cordially embraced the Gospel; they had manifested tender attachment for him; they had given themselves to God. But within a few short years they were allowing themselves to be led away and were now embracing doctrines designed to totally subvert the Gospel that Paul had imparted to them. Their behavior demonstrated their instability and inconsistency of character.

His amazement at the Galatians' reversal of character was heightened by the fact that he had presented to them a Gospel of free grace. Paul had expressed to them the utter hopelessness of humanity's attempt to earn God's love. The apostle informs them that the only thing a person could do was fling himself on God's mercy in an act of faith. Paul wondered, if a person could obtain the grace of God by the mere exercise of faith, why would they decide to work for that grace which is offered for free?

Paul's message of free grace is attacked by those preaching a Jewish version of Christianity. They insisted that if a person really wanted to please God she or he had to endure the ritual of circumcision, and obey the Mosaic Laws and regulations. "Every time a man performs a deed of the law...that was a credit entry in his account with God. They were teaching that it was necessary for a man to earn the favor of God." To Paul that was utterly impossible.[6]

17

Suppose you are offered a cashier's check for one million dollars and given the choice of accepting the money free of any strings, or working for the same amount. It would be considered the height of insanity to work for what one could have for free. Yet the Galatians were turning away from the Gospel of free grace to a gospel of works. No wonder Paul marvels at their reversal. Even today we find large numbers of professing Christians attempting to work their way into heaven and God's grace. They attempt to acquire God's love by works, when salvation is available by faith.

"I want you to know, brother, that the gospel I preached is not something that man made up" (1:11 NIV).

Throughout Paul's ministry he had many critics. Some argued that he was not a true apostle of Christ. They said this because he had not been a follower of the Lord while He was on earth. Therefore they argued that his teachings were designed by mistaken and misguided men. To these arguments Paul declared that his Gospel was not man-made nor did it come from men. It was not a Gospel of the good works of men, but of Jesus Christ. Paul's Gospel was not a message that he had learned from any man. It was not given by tradition or acquired in an educational institution. His Gospel was a revelation directly from his Lord, Jesus Christ.

"Revelation means a truth that is shared by God to [us], a truth that [we] never knew."[7] It is crucial to note this point, for Paul's call to preach the Gospel rested upon this single fact: Did Jesus Christ really reveal Himself and the truth of His death and resurrection to Paul or not? If Paul was lying, then he was not a true minister of the Gospel. He was a fraud, a deceiver, a man who viewed the ministry only as a profession to provide a livelihood and to secure honor and power over people. If those who criticized him could not see that there was a change in Paul, he knew that something miraculous had occurred in his life. His message of destruction had been replaced by grace and faith in the Lord Jesus Christ. The change in his life and message was

18

due to his encounter with Christ, therefore he had no doubts about the authenticity of his apostleship.

"On the contrary, they saw that I had been entrusted with the task of preaching the gospel to the Gentiles, just as Peter had been to the Jews" (2:7-8 NIV).

There will always be some who are swayed by new-fangled views and ideas. Yet there are those who remain true to their commitment, and stand fast in what they are taught. This was the case with the leaders of the Galatian church. They did not agree with their teaching as the Judaizers had hoped. These leaders stood firm and championed the call and Gospel of Christ. They were assured that God had called Paul to preach to the Gentiles (the uncircumcised) in the same manner that God had called Peter to the Jews (the circumcised). Both Paul and Peter championed the truth, that God gives to every person a particular task.

Paul's apostleship was not merely one of his declaration. His apostleship was also being affirmed by the other apostles at Jerusalem. These leaders of the Jerusalem church—James, Peter, and John—these great pillars of the church were standing together with Paul and proclaiming that salvation by grace through faith alone was the true Gospel. They further proclaimed that all ministers should minister to the poor, not just to the middle classes and wealthy.

Christians should never be detoured from their commitment to assigned tasks from Christ. Regardless of the criticism, Christians must maintain their integrity to their calling.

"But the fruit of the Spirit is love, joy, peace, patience, kindness, goodness, faithfulness, gentleness and self-control. Against such things there is no law" (5:22-23 NIV).

Here the Apostle Paul speaks of the **fruit** and not the fruits of the Spirit. Fruit is singular and not plural. There is only one fruit of the Holy Spirit. When the Holy Spirit lives in a person, all the traits listed in verses 22-23 are present. The life of the Christian is not composed of one trait but of all the traits mentioned. The

19

Holy Spirit produces all of these traits in the life of the believer.

The greatest of the traits mentioned is *agape* (love), because it is the very love possessed by God. Agape is the love demonstrated by our Saviour on the Cross at Calvary. It is love for the unlovely, the love given by God to all of us—sinners and enemies of God.

Another trait of the fruit of the Spirit is joy. It is represented by deep inner peace, gladness and assurance in the life of the believer. Joy indicates a cheerful heart which leads to cheerful behavior.

The trait of peace is the force that binds us to God and the Christian community; but it is not a peace of escapism. It is a peace that is the result of God's reconciliation; God is reconciled to people and people to God.

Longsuffering is the trait which encompasses the virtues of patience, perseverance, and steadfastness. J.B. Lyles points out that the trait of longsuffering never strikes back and is a fruit of God's very own Spirit, a fruit that is to be in the life of the believer.[8] Gentleness is a trait which demonstrates a concern for others and their feelings. This trait illustrates sympathy and empathy with those who are suffering and struggling.

"Brother, if someone is caught in a sin, you who are spiritual should restore him gently. But watch yourself, or you also may be tempted" (6:1 NIV).

The King James version of this Scripture says, "Brethren, if a man be overtaken in a fault..." Here the apostle emphasizes that the person he is talking about is of like passions, desires and urges as ourselves; one who walks and lives in the flesh just like each of us does; one who faces the exact same temptation that we do.

The question that each Christian must answer is: How must we respond to a brother or sister who has succumbed to temptation? In what spirit and attitude should we approach this person? Should we ignore, criticize, shame, dismiss or isolate her or him? Note that Paul does not specify any particular sin. It could be big or small, despicable or acceptable (to us), serious or innocent, harmful or harmless.[9]

To be overtaken unexpectedly, whether we want to acknowledge it or not, it is a possibility that all of us could experience. But what is extremely important is the response of our Christian colleagues. The Scripture is explicitly clear: Christians are to restore their fallen brothers and sisters, to help lead them back to the right path.

The Apostle Paul cautions us that there is a right and wrong way to bring about restoration. We are challenged to restore our fallen brothers and sisters in the spirit of gentleness. The failure to respond in the proper attitude could cause the person to be lost to our fellowship and to God. Therefore, we should be aware that the task of restoration is of extreme importance to brothers and sisters who have been overtaken. Does the church realize that this is our ministry? The ministry of God? The ministry of restoration? It is the ministry to which God has called us. We are to restore men and women to the kingdom of God and the fellowship of His Church.[10]

While not specifying any particular sin, Paul does specify those who should be the instruments of restoration—*those who are spiritual.* Not everyone can bring about restoration. The characterization of the spiritual is expressed in Galatians 5:22-23. Those who are spiritual bear the fruit expressed in the Scripture. The fruit of the Spirit is love, joy, peace, patience, kindness, faithfulness, gentleness, goodness, and self-control.

The process of restoration must be done in meekness. This approach is desperately needed. In the last few years we have seen servants of the Lord overtaken by temptations. But in many of these incidents the approach to those overtaken was anything but a spirit of meekness. Instead, a spirit of arrogance, criticism, rumor, slander, super-spirituality and a holier-than-thou attitude was shown. In many cases the intent was not restoration but destruction.

How often we forget ourselves in the process of restoration. Ask yourselves: Do I stop to think that this fallen brother or sister could be me? How would I want to be approached? For we also may be tempted and overtaken by sin. Therefore, we should extend to our fallen brother or sister the love and concern we would want for ourselves. To be sure, we must discuss and deal with the sins which brought our brother or sister to this fallen state, but the discussion must be with the fallen Christian and not the community. We should seek to bring the fallen back into fellowship and make them aware that they are loved, forgiven and accepted.

"...*People reap what they sow*" (6:7, OAB).

Perhaps few people impact our society as do teachers. They are important both to society and God. Within the church the position of teacher is of paramount importance to the development of the church and its members. In the verse under consideration, Paul outlines the responsibility of students to their teachers. Each of us is a student—learning something from somebody.

Paul speaks of our responsibility to the teacher: "Let him that is taught in the word communicate unto him that teacheth in all good things" (6:6). Our responsibility is not merely financial, but also to communicate and share in the ministry of our teachers. We are challenged to share with the teacher "in all good things." This sharing involves the following: being present when the teacher teaches, being attentive to learn what the teacher teaches, participating in discussions, communicating to others what has been taught, giving financial support to the teaching ministry, and encouraging others to attend the teaching sessions.

The focus and primary responsibility of the Bible teacher is to impart the Word of God. The learners should assure themselves that what they are learning is in fact the Word of God.

Students should do good to their teachers because of the consequences. Instead of being supportive of the teaching ministry, many believers are in fact critics. They fail to understand that by attacking the teacher, they could be attacking God. When Paul says, "God is not mocked," (6:7) he is saying God is not someone you turn your nose up to. When the Galatians were shunning God's ministers they were rejecting God. Thus if a person sows rejection he will assuredly reap rejection. The list of what one can reap for ill-sown seed is perhaps endless. Those who sow to their human nature (the flesh), will reap death and judgment.

Those believers who sow to the Spirit, reap the blessing of the Spirit, life everlasting. In this world believers find fullness in the fruit of the Spirit—love, joy, peace, longsuffering, kindness, goodness, faithfulness, gentleness, and self-control. These are the blessings of those who sow to the Spirit.

SCRIPTURE FOCUS

GALATIANS 1:1 Paul, an apostle, (not of men, neither by man, but by Jesus Christ, and God the Father, who raised him from the dead;)

2 And all the brethren which are with me, unto the churches of Galatia:

3 Grace be to you and peace from God the Father, and from our Lord Jesus Christ,

4 Who gave himself for our sins, that he might deliver us from this present evil world, according to the will of God and our Father:

5 To whom be glory for ever and ever. Amen.

6 I marvel that ye are so soon removed from him that called you into the grace of Christ unto another gospel:

7 Which is not another; but there be some that trouble you, and would pervert the gospel of Christ.

8 But though we, or an angel from heaven, preach any other gospel unto you than that which we have preached unto you, let him be accursed.

2:20 I am crucified with Christ: nevertheless I live; yet not I, but Christ liveth in me: and the life which I now live in the flesh I live by the faith of the Son of God, who loved me, and gave himself for me.

5:1 Stand fast therefore in the liberty wherewith Christ hath made us free, and be not entangled again with the yoke of bondage.

2 Behold, I Paul say unto you, that if ye be circumcised, Christ shall profit you nothing.

3 For I testify again to every man that is circumcised, that he is a debtor to do the whole law.

4 Christ is become of no effect unto you, whosoever of you are justified by the law; ye are fallen from grace.

5 For we through the Spirit wait for the hope of righteousness by faith.

6 For in Jesus Christ neither circumcision availeth any thing, nor uncircumcision; but faith which worketh by love.

SCRIPTURE SEARCH

Match the Columns.

1. Source of Paul's apostleship (1:1)

A. Another Gospel

2. Source of a curse (1:8-9)

B. Love

3. Source of Paul's life (2:20)

C. Christ

4. Source of liberty (5:1)

D. Jesus Christ and God

5. Faith works but by…(5:6)

E. Made us free

The African American Connection

1. Culture rejection?

There is a parallel between the Galatians' rejection of the Gospel's fundamental truths and the willingness of many African Americans to cast aside their teachings, heritage, cultural identity and sense of community in order to lose themselves in an alien culture. They believe that if somehow they cast off their negritude, the larger society will think them more acceptable. Just as Esther forgot her cultural background for the pleasure of the king's palace and almost lost her life and the lives of her people, so it is that many of us reject the teachings of the love of God, self, family, and community.

As the Galatians were entangled in the new teaching of works by persons posing as their friends, so many African Americans are casting aside their cultural involvement in the church, because the alien society has lulled them to sleep with songs of their difference. "You are different from other members of your group," they say. Thus these sons and daughters of sharecroppers, day laborers, and domestics reject the religious instruction of their fathers as so much cultural baggage.

In spite of the many blessings African Americans have received, due in no small part to the prayers and sufferings of our forefathers and-mothers many of us have fooled ourselves into believing that we have achieved success on our own merit.

2. Salvation by works?

The Galatians were taught that they could achieve salvation by works only. So too many African Americans believe they can soothe their consciences by good works. The old time religion which was good enough for their fathers and mothers, is not good enough for them. They reject the teachings of their ancestors, thereby also rejecting their foreparents' God.

Galatians had regressed from Paul's teachings, designed to take them from earth to glory, and in a similar manner many African Americans have rejected the future for the present and life for death. Perhaps African Americans will gain the wisdom learned by the experience of the Prodigal Son. He realized that his hope was not in the pig pen but in his father's house. Therefore he decided to return to his cultural roots. The hope for us as a people is not in the alien teachings which reject our cultural heritage, our relations with the God of our parents, our sense of family and sense of community. Our hope is in a return to those cultural principles that sustained us in times of trial and trouble.

3. What do you think?

A. Is it right to impose one's cultural, social, religious or denominational beliefs and ideas upon others?

B. Should one reject one's heritage to seek the approval of others?

C. In what ways would you respond to the statement, "For African Americans, forgiveness is a unifying force." In what ways could this be applied to your church, your leaders, your family or your community?

EPHESIANS:
A Letter of Encouragement

Dr. Mary Carr
Ephesians 1:1-4; 2:8-10; 6:10-20

THE CITY
Location

Just at the mouth of Cayster, a large seaport in the Roman area of Asia Minor, stands the great seaport of Ephesus. Originally named Ionia for its early Greek inhabitancy, influence and culture, Ephesus was the first "urban" center of Asia and one of the two leading cities on Asia's west coast. Its capital, Pergamon, is located 90 miles to the North.

Ephesus is bordered by Izmir (formally Smyrna) to the North and Turkey (Miletus) to the South. Some 200 miles west of Ephesus, across the Aegean Sea, is Athens, which is connected by an isthmus to the city of Corinth. Corinth was noted for its commercial and military power.

Though a thriving center of commerce, Ephesus was perhaps better known as a haven for philosophers, poets, artists and orators. Corinth was actually a rival city whose inhabitants also excelled in these disciplines.[1] The Apostle Paul worked in these areas for extended periods of time as an evangelist and organizer of churches.

Many of Paul's converts came from pagan or non-Christian and non-Jewish religions. The leading religion of Ephesus was the worship of Diana, the goddess of fertility. An oriental cult that worshiped Artemis, the Greek version of the Roman Diana, also thrived.[2] Indeed, a structure built in Artemis's honor, the fifth of its kind on this site, was erected in 330 B.C. This idol is counted as one of the Seven Great Wonders of the World.[3]

27

An abundance of trade revolved around this cult cluster. Tourists and worshipers made pilgrimages to Ephesus to purchase various types of souvenirs, especially silver. The craftsmen made their living by creating images of the Meteroil Stone, the image of Diana "fallen from heaven" (Acts 19:35). In Acts 19:23-27 (NIV), the silversmith Demetrius expressed concern about the Apostle Paul's impact on his trade.

History

The evolution of Ephesian civilization has been a continued source of fascination for historians. According to J. Finegan, the first settlers of Ephesus were Carians and Leleges, but they were later expelled by Androclus, the prince of Athens. Androclus led the Greek colonization of Ephesus around 1100 B.C., and over time, the Greeks (Ionians) have been credited with the founding of Ephesus.[4]

At the time of the founding of the Christian Church in Ephesus, the population had grown to approximately 500,000 inhabitants. Paul's three missionary journeys throughout the Roman Empire, which began in Ephesus around 53 A.D. (Acts 18:7-8, 19-21), firmly established him as the one who introduced Christianity to Ephesus. Given the popularity of Diana worship, much evangelistic work was necessary. Paul left Aquila and his wife, Priscilla in Ephesus so that he would continue his ministry on the road (Acts 18:24-26). He returned to Ephesus after two years to preach and teach in the synagogues, working to persuade Jews and Greeks. Many miracles were done, and souls were saved (Acts 19:8-13).

THE LETTER

Structure

The Apostle Paul's epistle to the Ephesians can be viewed according to the following organization:

1. Introduction: Address and Greeting (1:1—2:10)
2. The Converted and Unconverted (2:11-22)
3. The Church and Duties of Its Members (3:1—6:1-9)
4. The Christian's Warfare (6:10-18)
5. Conclusion (6:19-23)

Analysis

Ephesians is in the group of Paul's epistles that include Colossians, Philemon and Philippians, collectively called "The Prison Epistles." Evidently, this glorious epistle was addressed to the church in Ephesus (Acts 19), and may also have been intended for circulation to the neighboring churches. "He wrote this letter about A.D. 61 from prison in Rome, the first of his so-called prison epistles, and sent it to Asia together with Colossians and Philemon."[5]

1. Introduction: Address and Greeting (1:1—2:10)

The epistle begins with Paul's usual salutation and thanksgiving, followed by a prayer of intercession. It is addressed to the saints of God: "The word saints means 'holy people'...that which belongs to God in a special way, that which is marked off for God. So the word 'saints' here means 'God's people.'"[6] "For we are God's workmanship, created in Christ Jesus to do good works..." (2:10, NIV).

The phrase "in Ephesus" is missing from Ephesians 1:1 in some of the earliest and most reliable manuscripts. Thus, a specific destination is not provided for this letter.

Paul, in intercessory prayer, gives thanks because both the Jew and the Gentile are made alive in Christ Jesus. Jews and Gentiles are equal in the promise that God made to Abraham (Genesis 12:2-3, 7). Christ being the Head of the Church has created one body:

"Remember that at that time you (Gentile) were separated from Christ, excluded from citizenship in Israel and foreigners to the covenants of the promise, without hope and without God in the world. But now in Christ Jesus, you who once were far away have been brought near through the blood of Christ" (Ephesians 2:12-13).

Although not the same, under the new covenant, God made us equal.

2. The Converted and the Unconverted (2:11-22)

Ephesians gives no clue concerning any specific problem in the Ephesian congregation. However, Paul does say that most of the Ephesian congregation were Gentile converts, though the number of Jewish Christians was not small (Acts 19:10, 17). Because their conversion took place in A. D. 55 and Ephesians was written in A. D. 61, the people of the congregation were relatively young in the Lord when they read Paul's letter for the first time.[7]

Paul encourages the converted Gentiles and Jews to understand that they were united in Christ. They were reconciled to God and therefore to one another. "Separated from Christ" is used to describe the Gentiles' alienation from God's people, God's promises, and the hope of redemption in Christ and from God Himself. Paul expounds on the importance of redemption. He emphasizes that Christ broke down the wall between the Jews and the Gentiles:

"Consequently, you are no longer foreigners and aliens, but fellow citizens with God's people and members of God's household, built on the foundation of the prophets, with Christ Jesus as the chief cornerstone" (2:19-20, NIV).

Since the wall or partition has been broken down for the Gentiles, "they are new creatures in Christ." Therefore, they are to put "...away falsehood, let everyone speak the truth with his/her neighbor, for we are members of one another. Be angry but do not sin; do not let the sun go down on your anger, and give no opportunity to the devil" (4:25-27; The New Oxford Annotated Bible).

3. The Church and Duties of Its Members (3:1—6:1-9)

The mystery of Christ has been revealed to Paul, now a prisoner. It is the dispensation (time or age) of the grace of God. This revelation led Paul to "preach among the Gentiles the unsearchable riches of Christ" (3:8). As noted, this mystery was latent in Old Testament typology and prophecy but not revealed, and was foretold by Christ (Matthew 16:18) The mystery involves the hidden richness of God's grace, to include in the Church both Jews and Gentiles.[8]

In chapter four, Paul calls the members of the church to practice the unity that God has created:

"Make every effort, to keep the unity of the Spirit through the bond of peace. There is one body and one Spirit—just as you were called to one hope when you were called—one Lord, one faith, one baptism; one God and Father of all, who is over all and through all" (4:4-6, NIV).

The Jews and Gentiles are no longer separated by worship rituals, but all are expected to worship in the same manner and have the same hope, faith and baptism.

Paul also speaks of the Church as the body of Christ, edified or built up by the various gifts of its members. He admonishes the members of their duties as Christians:

"Be imitators of God, therefore, as dearly loved children and live a life of love, just as Christ loved us and gave himself up for us as a fragrant offering and sacrifice to God. But among you there must not be even a hint of sexual immorality, or any kind of impurity, or of greed, because these are improper for God's holy people...for you were once in darkness but now you are light in the Lord" (5:1-3, 8, NIV).

Paul's moral instructions to the Ephesians (6:1-9) seems to be in concert dialogue with some important material in Colossians 3, in which parents, slaves and masters are addressed. The injunction of the Bible to families is to cause them to reflect Christ: "Colossians requires total obedience to parents since this is a Christian duty. Ephesians requires obedience to parents, provided this is in the Lord, that is consistent with Christian commitment."[9] (Mitton, p. 210).

31

For early Christianity in general, the institution of slavery was regarded as a fixed part of society.[10] On the other hand, slavery is not given theological sanction. However, the church is to pattern its commitment to the cause of Christ after the example of slaves' loyalty and commitment to their masters. "The same sincere Christ-honoring conduct is enjoined upon masters as upon slaves...They are to act in the light of Christ's mastery over their lives, bearing in mind that there is no respect of persons or earthly position with [Christ]" (Acts 10:34). They are to be servants for the cause of Christ.

4. The Christian Warfare (6:10-18)

The Christian, in his walk, inevitably engages the opposition and spiritual resistance of Satan and his hosts. Paul admonishes the saints to "be strong in the Lord, and in the power of his might" (6:10, KJV). Christians are encouraged to put on the armor of God in order to withstand the onslaughts of the evil one. Reference is also made to the armor of God in the Old Testament (Isaiah 11:5; 59:17). The word of God is to be the armament of Christians.[11]

The battle is serious, for it is not against human agencies, but against the supernatural powers which inhabit the cosmos: "For we wrestle not against flesh and blood, but against principalities, against powers, against rulers of the darkness of this world, against spiritual wickedness in high places" (Ephesians 6:12, KJV).

The Christian's confidence is made firm in the knowledge that all these are subject to Christ.[12] A glimpse of the Roman soldiers while a prisoner certainly may have inspired Paul, metaphorically speaking, to be prepared for Christian warfare against evil. Christians are to stand firm in the Word of God and use the Word as an offensive weapon against the incursion of Satan, just as Jesus used the Word against Satan when He was tempted in the wilderness (Matthew 4:1ff.)

5. Conclusion (6:19-24)

To close the letter, Paul said that he would keep in touch through Tychicus, his faithful friend, so that he could keep the Ephesians informed about his welfare. He closes with a benediction: "Grace be with all them that love our Lord Jesus Christ in sincerity. Amen."

MAJOR THEMES

Biblical research has revealed that there were no particular problems, but there were doctrinal heresies threatening the neighborhood churches. Jensen describes problems in some of the local churches: internal strife (Colossians); false accusations (1 Corinthians); and false doctrine (2 Corinthians and Galatians). He also suggests that perhaps there were individual problems in the Ephesian church.

Therefore Paul wrote this new letter to the church: a) to show a relationship between Christ and his church for assurance, and to provide correction to young Christians maturing in the Lord; b) to admonish young Christians to grow spiritually in the Lord, understanding what was expected of them; and c) to explain what it means to walk in the Light of Christ. Paul was inspired to address this epistle to the basic needs of the young converts for spiritual growth.

The primary truths that the Lord is trying to communicate through the writer to the reader is God's redemptive purpose for the world. The themes stressed in this writing are: a) God's divine election, b) propitiation/reconciliation and c) the Church as the body of Christ.

Election

First, in the Old Testament, God made agreement with Abraham: "I will make thee a great nation, and I will bless thee...and in thee shall all families of the earth be blessed" (Genesis 12:2a-3b). This was an everlasting covenant with Abraham and his descendants.

33

The Gentiles had no access to the covenant which promised salvation. They were outside of the commonwealth of Israel (2:11-13, KJV). They were without hope, estranged and alienated from God. But the mystery was revealed to Paul that in the beginning "God chose us (Gentiles) in Him before the foundation of the world...God destined us in love to be His sons [and daughters] through Jesus Christ" (Ephesians 1:4-5). Paul was inspired to emphasize that God's purpose was to "...set forth in Christ a plan for the fullness of time, to unite all things in him, things in heaven and things on earth" (1:9b-10, OAB).

"In Him (Christ) we have redemption through his blood, the forgiveness for our trespasses..." (1:7, OAB). Election becomes effective when one who was chosen before the foundation of the world, comes to Christ salvation.

Propitiation and Reconciation
Propitiation/reconciliation is a profound theme in Ephesians. The barriers between God and humankind and those between fellow human beings are broken. Jesus became the propitiation or sacrifice for the sins of humankind and reconciled humankind back to God through His death and resurrection. Jesus closed the chasm:

"For he (Jesus) is our peace, who hath made us both one, and has broken down the dividing wall of hostility by abolishing in flesh the law of commandments and ordinances that he might create in himself a new [person] in the place of two, so making peace, and might reconcile us both to God in one body through the cross, thereby bringing the hostility to an end" (2:14-16, OAB).

Jesus broke the system of racism, classism, sexism and oppression by making all one in Christ. "There is neither Jew nor Greek, male nor female, bond nor free, but we are all one in Christ Jesus" (Galatians 3:28, KJV). The Gentiles are fellow heirs, members of the same body, and partakers of the promise in Christ Jesus through the Gospel.

34

The Church as Christ's Body

Finally, the prevailing theme is the Church as the body of Christ. Paul uses a profound metaphor when he describes the Church as Christ's body, making Christ Himself the Head. He calls Christ the "head of the body," indicating that Christ rules over and directs the Church as a person's head directs the body.

In Christ Jesus, Jews and Gentiles are now in a new community, the Church. Gentiles have now been given the opportunity to share in covenant with Israel (Genesis 12:2-3). The Jewish people were set apart by circumcision, but circumcision is no longer required to set God's people apart. It is not by rituals and traditions that one is saved, but by confession and acceptance, making Jesus Lord of our lives and bonding that relationship with love and unity in Christ.

In the church at Ephesus there were those who were oppressed racially and socially. Some were chastised for their religious difference. The Gentiles were non-Jewish, uncircumcised and from different origins. Before Christ, they were alienated from the commonwealth of Israel, "...excluded from citizenship in Israel and [were] foreigners to (or not included in) the covenants, without hope and without God in the world" (Ephesians 2:12). Non-Jews could neither participate in religious worship nor enter the temple courts beyond the wall. But Christ destroyed the "wall of hostility."

SCRIPTURE FOCUS

EPHESIANS 1:1 Paul, an apostle of Jesus Christ by the will of God, to the saints which are at Ephesus, and to the faithful in Christ Jesus:

2 Grace be to you, and peace, from God our Father, and from the Lord Jesus Christ.

3 Blessed be the God and the Father of our Lord Jesus Christ, who hath blessed us with all spiritual blessings in heavenly places in Christ:

4 According as he hath chosen us in him before the foundation of the world, that we should be holy and without blame before him in love:

2:8 For by grace are ye saved through faith; and that not of yourselves: it is the gift of God:

9 Not of works, lest any man should boast.

10 For we are his workmanship, created in Christ Jesus unto good works, which God hath before ordained that we should walk in them.

6:10 Finally, my brethren, be strong in the Lord, and in the power of his might.

11 Put on the whole armour of God, that ye may be able to stand against the wiles of the devil.

12 For we wrestle not against flesh and blood, but against principalities, against powers, against the rulers of the darkness of this world, against spiritual wickedness in high places.

13 Wherefore take unto you the whole armour of God, that ye may be able to withstand the evil day, and having done all, to stand.

14 Stand therefore, having your loins girt about you with truth, and having on the breastplate of righteousness;

15 And your feet shod with the preparation of the gospel of peace;

16 Above all, taking the shield of faith, wherewith ye shall be able to quench all the fiery darts of the wicked.

17 And take the helmet of salvation, and the sword of the Spirit, which is the word of God:

18 Praying always with all prayer and supplication the Spirit, and watching there-unto with all perseverance and supplication for all saints;

19 And for me, that utterance may be given unto me, that I may open my mouth boldly, to make known the mystery of the gospel,
20 For which I am an ambassador in bonds: that therein I may speak boldly, as I ought to speak.

SCRIPTURE SEARCH

1. When were Christians chosen by God? (Ephesians 1:4)
2. How is salvation experienced? (2:8)
3. What is the source of spiritual strength? (6:10)
4. Who are our spiritual enemies? (6:12)
5. Besides putting on spiritual armor, what else must Christians be sure to do? (6:18)

The African American Connection

One of the truths that exists for African Americans is racial injustice. We are still experiencing this evil which is manifested in alienation and isolation. The spiritual wall of hostility has been torn down by Christ, and we are all one in Him. But, "the natural wall" remains.

1. How do we respond to racial injustice as Christians?
2. How do we see ourselves in this natural and spiritual warfare?
3. What does it mean to put on the full armor of God and fight against these powers of darkness?
4. What elements of the Sword of the Spirit will prove useful in this battle?
5. How can we re-educate, equip and empower ourselves for survival and victory in this deadly struggle?

PHILIPPIANS:
A Letter of Joy

Dr. Bennie Goodwin
Philippians 1:1-4, 9-11; 3:13-14; 4:1-8

THE CITY

If, like John, you were banished to the island of Patmos, or to Cyprus, Rhodes or one of the other islands in the Mediterranean Sea, what four books would you take with you? My choices would be the *Bible, The Prophet* by Kahlil Gibran, *Strength to Love* by Martin Luther King, Jr. and *Disciplines of the Spirit* by Dr. Howard Thurman.[1]

If I could take only two "books" from the Bible, they would be the Psalms and Philippians. Paul's letter to the Philippians is delightful. It is only four chapters long and full of love, gratitude and personal concern.

Of course, if I had lived in the first century I would have volunteered to go on that second missionary journey. I would like to have been there when Paul heard the call "to come over into Macedonia and help us" (Acts 16:9). It would have been so exciting to join Paul, Silas, Timothy and Luke as they sailed from Troas, made a stop on the island of Samothrace and landed in the seaport town of Neapolis (Acts 16:11).[2]

After having travelled the 175 miles from Troas to Neapolis folks probably would threaten to leave in order to stop me from exploring the markets, and other interesting sights.[3]

But I wouldn't want to travel the 10 miles to Philippi without some company. On the other hand, I might be tempted to slip over to one of the other bustling seaport towns like Amphipolis, the capital city of Thessalonica, or maybe down to Athens or

Corinth. Anyway, I'd better stay with the group. Luke is so anxious for us to see Philippi, his hometown.[4]

And what a sight! The whole city is surrounded by mountains. On the West is Pangaens and on the East is cone-shaped Orbelos. Now we are slowly descending about 500 feet through the Symbolon Hills into the city proper.[5] Luke is so excited. He tells us that the ancient Phoenician city kind of sprung up around a well or series of wells called *Krenides* which means fountains.[6] Later, gold mines were discovered here and the city became the financial and military headquarters for Philip II of Macedonia. Later his son Alexander the Great launched his campaign to conquer the world from this very spot.

Philip gave the city his name and it was here that Octavius and Anthony defeated Brutus and Cassius in 42 B.C. after they had assassinated Julius Caesar.[7] This famous city is strategically located on the Egnatian Road that connects Asia with Europe. Eventually this road leads to Rome, the capital of the world, where Paul wrote his letter to the Philippian church.[8]

THE CHURCH

Well, we entered Philippi and went down by the Gandites River where Paul heard that some people were meeting for prayer. As it turned out, we met a rich, attractive sister named Lydia. She wasn't saved but she worshiped God and when Paul told her about Jesus she accepted Him as her Saviour.[9]

She was a really nice lady and invited us to her house. It was wonderful because we had not made any other living arrangements. Luke might have had a home here at one time but he didn't bring it up, so neither did we.

As we went back and forth to worship "down by the riverside," another young sister started following us. Every day she said the same thing: "these men are servants of the most high God" (Acts 16:17).

At first, the free publicity was good, but then it got so obnoxious that one day Paul turned suddenly and cast the evil spirit out of the girl. And to our amazement she was cured. Right on the spot, the demon left her.

At the time, I thought that was wonderful. But as it turned out this girl was working for some men in town telling-you know, fortunes, reading palms, doing roots, that kind of stuff. Talk about upset, these brothers were so mad about the girl being cured that they had Paul and Silas arrested, beaten and thrown into solitary confinement. The situation was so bad that the Lord had to step in. An earthquake struck. Yes, an earthquake. I won't give you all the details. You can read about them in Luke's letter to Theophilus (Acts 1:1; 16:1-40). But the prison guard who beat Paul and Silas ended up getting saved—he and his whole family.

Soon after that incident we left Philippi and went on to our next stop. So I still got to see Amphipolis, Apollonia, Thessalonica and a lot of other interesting places (Acts 17:1).

THE LETTER

Dr. Hammonds mentions in his chapter on Colossians that many of Paul's letters have a simple two-part outline. They consist of a first section on doctrinal principles followed by a section on practical Christian living. Paul's letter to the Philippian church is a personal passage and does not follow this two-part outline. It is more like a letter you or I might write to our friends. After a greeting, we basically write as thoughts come to us.

But at the feet of Gamaliel, Paul had put in many years of study. He had trained his mind to think logically and systematically, and so even when writing a personal letter he could not just ramble on and on. There is a structure even to this letter to his friends and spiritual family in Philippi.

Structure

1. Paul's Prison Experience: Joy in Suffering (1:1-30)
2. Paul's Pastoral Expectations: Joy in Service (2: 1-30)
3. Paul's Personal Expressions: Joy in Submission (3:1—4:23)

41

Analysis
1. Paul's Prison Experience: Joy in Suffering (1:1-30)

Joy is one of the themes for which this letter is known. Although Paul is a prisoner and has been for a while, he does not mope and grope. There's not a lot of criticizing and complaining, there are no indications of depression or invitations to a pity party. The theme is Joy with a capital *J*.

The letter begins with Paul admitting that he is a prisoner. But from his house-prison he sends out grace, peace thanksgiving, joy, confidence, love and affection (1:1-8).

He is not begging for prayer to "hold on and hold out." No, the imprisoned is praying for the free. He is praying that their love, knowledge and judgment may grow, and that they may be excellent, sincere and productive (1:9-11).

Then he begins to tell the Philippians how wonderful it is to be a preacher and a prisoner in Rome at the same time. No, everybody is not patting him on the back and complimenting him for his Christian message. In fact, some preachers are preaching Christ to make his life more difficult. But he's happy that Christ is being preached (1:18). Yes, like every normal prisoner he hopes to be released (1:19). In fact, he's getting on in age and because of all the travelling, the trouble, trials and tribulations (2 Corinthians 11:26), he sometimes feels like going on home to be with the Lord. But then he decides to stay on earth a while longer to help more people in their Christian walk. The famous verse in this chapter is "for to me to live is Christ and to die is gain" (Philippians 1:21). The Living Bible translates it like this: "For to me, living means opportunities for Christ, and dying—well that's better yet!"

Paul is not denying that he is suffering and that his suffering is real, unwanted, sometimes undeserved and painful. But he believes that Christian suffering is unavoidable (1:29). He is convinced that the symbol of Christianity is not a big car, a big house, or a big bank account. The symbol of Christianity is a cross. Therefore, Paul says in effect, if I am going to follow Christ, I must follow Him to the Cross. And as He suffered, so must I. We have been given the privilege not only of trusting Him but also of suffering for Him (1:29). Paul would perhaps have loved the way Thomas Shepherd expressed it:

Must Jesus bear the cross alone,
And all the world go free?
No, there's a cross for everyone,
And there's a cross for me.

Now Paul was no masochist; he did not love pain or like to suffer. But he loved the fact that suffering for Christ made him known, resulted in people's lives being changed and deepened Paul's hope of the Resurrection. Thomas Shepherd's hymn continues:

The consecrated cross I'll bear
Til death shall set me free,
And then go home my crown to wear
For there's a crown for me.

2. Paul's Pastoral Expectations: Joy in Service (2:1-30).

Paul was writing to people he knew, in a church he founded. We don't know for sure, but there seems to have been a little disunity and maybe a little competition in the Philippian church (2:1-4; 4:1-3). So Paul encouraged the leadership to make his joy complete by uniting their minds around the challenge of humble service (2:1-4).

And then he quotes what we believe was a first century hymn about Jesus. To get the essence of it, you should read it several times in as many translations as you can find. I am so glad Paul wrote this letter because nowhere in Scripture is this understanding of God becoming a human being expressed more profoundly. Thank God for Philippians 2:5-11 and John 1:1-18. Even after we read it, study it and meditate on it, it's still a mystery how divinity can become humanity; how an invisible God can become a visible man. But thank God for the light that these passages shed on the subject.

With Jesus as our example, Paul calls us to a partnership-ministry. God saves us but He asks us to complete the salvation process by our humble, diligent, cheerful and light-giving service to others (Philippians 2:12-15).

Paul closes this section of his letter by honoring two of his faithful ministry partners—Timothy and Epaphroditus. Timothy was probably saved through Paul's ministry (2:25) and served with him and in his place in many cities and churches. We can tell that he loves Timothy dearly.

Epaphroditus seems to be a "local boy" from Philippi who has made good. The Philippian congregation sent him to deliver some gifts to Paul and to serve as their hands, feet, mind and heart. In the course of serving Paul in Rome, Epaphroditus became seriously ill. He was so sick Paul thought he might die. Somehow the Philippians heard about it, so Paul sent this lovely little letter back by Epaphroditus to assure the church that Epaphroditus had carried out his assignment and was now returning to them in good health. Paul encouraged the church to receive their "ambassador" back like the hero he was (2:25-30).

It is interesting to see how age, experience and suffering softens us and develops our sensitivities. When Paul picked himself up off the Damascus Road, I don't believe he could have possibly written such a beautiful, tender and touching tribute to two unsung biblical heroes. We can almost feel the lump in his throat, the sweat on his palms and the tears in his eyes as he writes or dictates this part of the letter. It reminds us what they said about Jesus at Lazarus's tomb—"Oh how he loved him!" (John 11:36)

3. Paul's Personal Expressions: Joy in Submission (3:1—4:23)
In the final part of this lovely letter, Paul begins with a couple of sentences, warning his spiritual family of the dangerous Judaizers. These were folk who dogged Paul's footsteps like the Pharisees and scribes did Jesus. Paul went from city to city preaching and teaching that we are saved by God's grace when we put our trust in God, through Jesus Christ (Ephesians 2:8-9).

After Paul left the city, the Judaizers followed him, teaching that Paul was right, but only partially right. They said, yes we are saved by faith *plus* by keeping the Mosiac Laws. In other words, non-Jews could become Christians by trusting God through Jesus *and* Moses.

Not only did Paul believe their doctrine was wrong, he believed their motives were wrong, and he said so in very graphic language. He called them a religious mafia, a pack of street dogs, and a band of meat cutters. Sounds like he almost hated these folk, not personally but for the damage they caused.

In addition to contradicting Paul's teaching, they often tried to discredit him personally by saying that he was neither an authentic Jew nor a Christian.

We can give them credit for forcing Paul to tell us things about himself that we would have never known otherwise (Philippians 3:1-21).

In the first part of this passage, Paul sounds quite proud and conceited (3:3-6). But he lets us know that his great desire is to know Jesus (3:8-13). And that even after all he has done and is doing, he's still "bringing all of (his) energies to bear on this one thing...(and) straining to reach the end of the race and receive the prize...because of what Jesus did..." (3:13, LB). In the final verses of chapter three, he again asks his Philippian family to follow his example (3:15-21).

Love is one of the facts that keeps coming through in this letter. In the opening of the final chapter, he wrote, "O people of the church at Philippi, I love you and long to see you for you are my joy and my reward for my work" (4:1, LB). And then he calls the names of Euodia, Syntyche and Clement, and encourages them to love, help each other and work together in harmony. He encourages them to rejoice, not to worry, to be at peace, to think positively and to imitate his example (4:1-9).

He closes the letter as he started it, with thanksgiving. He began by thanking God for the Philippians (1:3) and he closes by thanking the Philippians for their kindness (4:10-18). He assures them that their ambassador, Epaphroditus has brought their gifts, and that as they have supplied his needs, from the abundance of God's great storehouse, their needs will be supplied (4:19).

THE PURPOSES

This letter was written by Paul to the church at Philippi for at least four reasons:

1. To thank them for their gifts and support.
2. To inform them about his life as a prisoner and the progress of the Gospel in Rome.
3. To challenge them to lives of joy, love and unity.
4. To prepare them for the return of Epaphroditus, the visits of Timothy, Paul, and the coming of the Day of the Lord.

1. Just Say "Thanks!"

"Thank you" is a wonderful phrase. It is one of my mother's "magic words" and my father's persistent dictums: "Always be thankful." Paul told the Thessalonians to give thanks in everything because that is what pleases God (1 Thessalonians 5:18). So here, Paul is putting his own principle into practice.

He thanks the Philippians for their gifts and support (Philippians 1:7; 4:10), for how they stuck with him through thick and thin, in good times and bad (4:14-26); and for sending Epaphroditus as their personal ambassador, to serve him. Paul is filled with gratitude to God and to the church members at Philippi for the blessings he has received. Every time they crossed his mind, his heart bubbled over with thanks (1:3).

2. Life as a Prisoner

It's important to keep in touch with those who love us, so Paul wrote this letter to let the Philippians know how he was doing. While he wanted them to pray that he would be delivered from his house-prison (1:19), he wanted them to know that the Lord was using him in prison for positive purposes.

Not only was he preaching the Gospel, but others were being influenced to preach also. In fact, the Good News of God's love and power through Christ was getting a hearing and response even in Caesar's palace (1:13). And there were now "saints" in Caesar's household (4:22). Paul said, "Yes, I'm a prisoner but the Gospel is being preached, people are getting saved; so I'm doing fine."

3. "Don't Fight, You're Christians!"

Paul wanted the saints to experience his quality of joy. He challenged them to be full of the Lord's joy (see 4:4, LB). Not just pleasure or happiness, which depends on circumstances, but the joy that the Lord gives (Galatians 5:22), which depends only on the quality of our relationship with Him.

Paul mentions the word "love" only four times (Philippians 1:4, 17; 2:1-2), but the love-aroma permeates the whole letter. Can there be any doubt that Paul loved Jesus and the Philippian saints? He encourages them to love each other as he loves them (2:1).

He wants them to be singleminded in their love (2:2) and to permit their love to motivate them to humble, Christ-like service (2:3-11).

Is it possible for Christians not to get side-tracked by differences? Is it possible for Christians to ignore people who try to introduce them to contrary teachings? Paul believed it was and encouraged the Philippian Christians not to be influenced by the false teachings of the Judaizers (3:1-2, 18-19), and to let their unity in Christ over-ride whatever personal differences they may be experiencing. He also encouraged the leaders of the church to work more harmoniously with each other and to experience the inner and outer peace that results from thoughts and conduct centered on the Lord and positive things (4:1-9).

4. Get Ready: Visitors Are Coming!

In Paul's day, the coming of important visitors were major events. Traveling was not a simple matter of hopping on a bus, train or airplane to a desired destination. Traveling the 800 miles between Rome and Philippi took a long time. And when one arrived at a destination it was not a simple matter of choosing between the Philippi Hilton, Marriott or Sheraton. Traveling took time and preparation. One of the purposes of this letter was to inform the church of Timothy's visit, Paul's possible visit and to tell them why Epaphroditus, their ambassador was returning at this time (2:19-30).

There is one other visit that Paul emphasized--the return of Jesus Christ. Paul expected Jesus to come any day. He called the event the "Day of Jesus Christ" (1:6, 10; 2:16). He looked forward to the day that the exalted Christ. When every knee would bow and every tongue confess that Jesus is Master of the universe (2:9-11). He was excited about the time when Jesus will return from heaven and our human bodies--now subject to pain and death, will be changed and live forever (3:20-21).

Are there Christians anywhere, who in their most serious moments do not look forward to a time of no crime, famine, sickness and death? That's the Day of Jesus Christ. It will be a sad day for unbelievers, but a happy, joyful, exciting and wonderful day for faithful, believing, serving Christians.

God's tomorrow is a day of Gladness,
And its joys shall never fade;

No more weeping, no more sense of sadness,
No more foes to make afraid.

God's Tomorrow, God's Tomorrow
Every cloud will pass away
At the dawning of that day;
God's Tomorrow, No more sorrow
For I know that God's Tomorrow
Will be better than today!
Alfred Ackley

There are four purposes for Paul's beautiful little letter: to say thanks, to tell how he was doing, to encourage Christian unity, and to prepare the Philippians for their special visitors.

THE CENTRAL MESSAGE
"Don't Worry, Be Happy" is the title of a popular song of the late '80s. On the surface it sounds like a poetic summary of Paul's letter to the Philippians. But is it really? Paul was not telling his favorite congregation to "be happy." He was telling them to be "full of Joy!" That's not the same, is it?

Christian Joy is Essential
Being "happy" depends on the "happenings." It depends on what's happening in our lives and the lives of those we love and care about. Our happiness depends on our outward circumstances. And with crime, violence, robbery and rape on the rise, who can be happy? With children starving, an increase in AIDS, child, spouse and drug abuse, who can be happy?

But if the question is, who can be filled with joy? Then that's a different question, isn't it? Because joy does not depend on outward circumstances. If it did, Paul could not have been filled with so much joy. He had been a world traveler but now his

49

movements were severely restricted. As a Roman citizen (Acts 16:37-38), freedom was his normal way of life, but now he is chained to Roman guards. How could he be happy? He couldn't, but he could be filled with joy!

Why? Because joy is an essential part of God's personality that He shares with us. Christian joy is not something we are born with. It is not a natural state or something we earn or achieve through discipline. It is an attribute of God, like grace (Philippians 1:2; 4:23) and peace (4:7). When we are born spiritually, the Lord reproduces in us certain of His own spiritual qualities (John 1:11-12; Galatians 5:22). One of those qualities is joy.

When we are saved (Acts 16:31), born again (John 3:3), redeemed (1 Peter 1:18) and forgiven (1 John 1:9), the Lord comes into our lives and brings joy with Him. Joy is then a part of our lives as it is of His. Christian joy is a gift and God is the source.

A little song we learned in Vacation Bible School reminds us:
If you want joy, real joy, wonderful joy,
Let Jesus come into your heart.

Your sins He'll wash away,
Your night He'll turn to day,
You life, He'll make it over anew.

If you want joy, real joy, wonderful joy,
Let Jesus come into your heart.

Christian Joy is Experience

Since joy is a permanent part of God's life and God is a permanent part of our lives, then rejoicing is automatic, isn't it? Or is it?

It wasn't automatic for the Philippians, was it? If it was, or why did Paul give them three direct reminders: "rejoice in the Lord"? (Philippians 3:1; 4:4)

Why don't we automatically rejoice in spite of racism, sexism and classism? Or in spite of our personal "troubles, trials and tribulations?" Joy is a fact, putting it into operation is an experience. Did you hear about the brother who lived as a beggar because he didn't know he had inherited a hundred thousand dollars? He was rich in *fact* but poor in *experience*. Paul was rich in fact *and* experience because he kept intimately connected with Jesus Christ, the source of his joy. In fact, Paul refers to Jesus no less than 64 times (KJV) in the 104 verses of Philippians.

The beggar, though rich, experienced poverty because he didn't keep in touch with his wealthy relative. We experience joy when through private devotions, public worship, and witness, and consistent obedience we keep in close connection with the Lord, the source of our joy (2:14-18; 4:4-9).

Christian Joy Is Expression

Paul not only possessed and experienced joy, he also expressed joy. Fortunately, the expression of joy does not always include going around wearing a "happy face." If it meant walking around with a pasted on smile all the time, many African American Christians would not qualify as full of joy.

Because of the constant pressure of being Black in America, most African American adults, including Christians, are usually on the verge of explosion. To offset the heat of the bomb beneath the surface, we major in "being cool." Even in church, we tend to look serious and even in our most joyful moments, we tend to look pained. Have you noticed that even when we're shouting or dancing or lifting our hands and voices in praise to God, we are more likely to be frowning than smiling?

Now we'll smile, laugh and even holler when Michael Jordan or Magic Johnson makes a basket, when someone gives us an unexpected gift or compliment, or when the preacher tells a truly funny story to drive home a point. But why don't we smile more in worship as an expression of our Christian joy?

Could it be we believe that the most authentic expressions of joy are not smiles, laughs or grins but instead involve maintaining a positive (1:12-18) and progressive (3:12-21) attitude in negative situations? Could it be that to express Christian joy means to believe in the love of God while being hated by people, to confirm the triumph of truth, honesty and justice in the midst of lying, cheating and inequality? To do your best and be your best, is this not joy?

To endure hostility and betrayal without becoming vindictive, to drink the bitter cup of insult and remain sweet in spirit, to be optimistic in pessimistic circumstances, to lift those who have fallen, is this not joy?

To work harder and be paid less because you're a woman, to be passed over for promotion and asked to train your boss, to keep your eyes on the goal and allow nothing to break your spirit, are these not authentic expressions of joy?

Christian Joy is Expectation

Because they were singing, playing instruments and dancing, the owners thought the slaves were happy. They weren't. To be a happy slave is a contradiction in terms. The happiness of slaves was a slave-owner's perspective, born of cruelty and insensitivity. The slaves could sing, play instruments and dance not because they enjoyed being slaves, but because they believed slavery was temporary. They had hope. They looked forward to the end of slavery.

Paul was full of joy because he looked forward to the day of his deliverance from his house-prison (1:19) and the expected "Day of Christ" (1:6, 10; 2:16; 3:21). On that Day he expected to be permanently delivered from his earthly life of trouble, toil and pain and to be with Christ, his Lord (1:23; 3:20-21). Our ancestors sang:

"I'm so glad trouble don't last always"
"Deep river my home is over Jordan"
"Steal away I ain't got long to stay here"
These are solemn songs but songs full of hope.

That's why we continue to sing, in spite of the negative images we see of ourselves on television and in the movies, in spite of overt and institutional racism, in spite of white on Black and Black on Black crime, in spite of gang violence, "red lining," race baiting, deteriorating schools, and neighborhoods.

We continue to sing (2:5-11), to work (2:7; 4:10), to pray (1:4, 9-11; 4:6), to endure (1:29; 4:12) and to love (1:9; 2:1-2; 4:1)-- looking forward to the day when the "Dream" of Dr. King, the "Day" of the Apostle Paul and the "kingdom" of Jesus Christ will become a reality.

Harder yet may be the fight.
Right won't always yield to might.
But if I'm right He'll fight my battle
I shall get home someday.

I do not know how long twill be
nor what the future holds for me
But this I know, if Jesus leads me
I shall get home someday.

SCRIPTURE FOCUS

PHILIPPIANS 1:1 Paul and Timotheus, the servants of Jesus Christ, to all the saints in Christ Jesus which are at Philippi, with the bishops and deacons:
2 Grace be unto you, and peace, from God our

Father, and from the Lord Jesus Christ.

3 I thank my God upon every remembrance of you,

4 Always in every prayer of mine for you all making request with joy,

9 And this I pray, that your love may abound yet more and more in knowledge and in all judgment;

10 That ye may approve things that are excellent; that ye may be sincere and without offence till the day of Christ;

11 Being filled with the fruits of righteousness, which are by Jesus Christ, unto the glory and praise of God.

3:13 Brethren, I count not myself to have apprehended: but this one thing I do, forgetting those things which are behind, and reaching forth unto those things which are before,

14 I press toward the mark for the prize of the high calling of God in Christ Jesus.

4:1 Therefore, my brethren dearly beloved and longed for, my joy and crown, so stand fast in the Lord, my dearly beloved.

2 I beseech Euodias, and beseech Syntyche, that they be of the same mind in the Lord.

3 And I entreat thee also, true yokefellow, help those women which laboured with me in the gospel, with Clement also, and with other my fellow labourers, whose names are in the book of life.

4 Rejoice in the Lord always: and again I say, Rejoice.

5 Let your moderation be known unto all men. The Lord is at hand.

6 Be careful for nothing; but in every thing by

prayer and supplication with thanksgiving let your requests be made known unto God.
7 And the peace of God, which passeth all understanding, shall keep your hearts and minds through Christ Jesus.
8 Finally, brethren, whatsoever things are true, whatsoever things are honest, whatsoever things are just, whatsoever things are pure, whatsoever things are lovely, whatsoever things are of good report, if there be any virtue, and if there be any praise, think on these things.

SCRIPTURE SEARCH

Let's play Bible Jeopardy, the answers are given, you provide the questions.
1. Timothy (1:1)
2. Philippians 1:9-11
3. God, in Christ Jesus (2:14)
4. Always (4:4)
5. Philippians 4:8

The African American Connection

What is the difference between happiness and joy?
A. Is the Lord the only source of joy? If so, why? If not, what are some other sources of joy?
B. Give two or three reasons why African American Christians should or should not be happy.
C. Give two or three reasons why African American Christians can be full of joy.

COLOSSIANS:
A Letter of Christ's Superiority

Dr. Kenneth Hammonds
Colossians 1:1-4, 12-20; 2:6-10

THE CITY
Location

The epistle of Paul to the Colossians was written around A.D. 60, to a city in Asia Minor named Colosse (ko-LOS-see). Colosse was about 100 miles east of the great city of Ephesus in Asia. This was the same general area of the seven churches of Asia mentioned in the Book of Revelation. It also was about 300 miles west of Tarsus, the city of the Apostle Paul's birth. The city of Colosse was located in a very fertile valley called the Lycus Valley which was surrounded by four mountain ranges. This fertile area was also known for its earthquakes. Colosse was surrounded by two other cities in the Lycus Valley that are mentioned the Book of Colossians, Herapolis and Laodicea (Colossians 4:13, 15). These three cities form an "L" shape in the Lycus Valley. (The interested student should refer to a Bible lands map in the back of a study Bible.)

History

Neither the founder of Colosse nor its early history are known, but the city was already in existence during the days of Xerxes of Persia, 485-465 B.C. (King Ahasuerus of the Book of Esther). In 401 B.C. the Greek historian Herodotus described Colosse as a "city inhabited and prosperous and great."[1] However, by the time of the Apostle Paul the city's competitors removed its influence as a major commercial power.

The Christian church in Colosse and perhaps all the churches in the Lycus Valley were most likely founded by Epaphas between 54-56 A.D. (1:7; 4:12-13; Philemon 23).[2] Also in the Book of Philemon there is mention of other leaders and individuals at the church in Colosse—Philemon, Apphia, Archippus, and Onesimus. The church met in Philemon's home (Philemon 2). The church at Colosse never had a great influence in the history of the early Christian church and in the 7 and 8th centuries it became deserted as a result of an earthquake. By the 12th century it had totally disappeared.

People

The people of the Lycus Valley and the surrounding areas were called the Phrygians (this part of Asia was called Phrygia.) The Phrygians worshiped many local deities as did most of the non-Christian world of that time. However, many Jews lived in this area. They were first transported there by Antiochus the Great (223-187 B.C.). By 62 B.C. there were more than 11,000 Jews in the Laodicea/Colosse area. The Jews prospered there and participated in the business endeavors of wool-dyeing and other commercial efforts. This area was of great influence and importance in the lives of the Jews in the 1st century A.D. According to Acts 2:10 there were Jews from Phrygia present on the Day of Pentecost.

THE LETTER

Journeys and Epistles of Paul

An understanding of the Pauline missionary journeys will bring even more light and life to the Colossian epistle. There are three recorded missionary journeys of Paul in the Book of Acts. The first was A.D. 46-48; the second was A.D. 50-52; and the third was AD 53-57. Acts 21—28 provide the history and background for the time of the writing of Colossians. At the end of his third missionary journey in Jerusalem, Paul was falsely accused and imprisoned and sent to Caesarea where he was a prisoner for approximately two years. In Caesarea, Paul made the appeal of his case to Caesar and was sent to Rome. On his way to Rome he was shipwrecked, but God protected him and he made it safely to Rome. In Acts 28, he is in his own rented house and under house arrest until the appeal of his case to Caesar (Nero). Some conservative Bible scholars believe that Paul was released in A.D. 62 and that he went on to minister on a fourth missionary journey, possibly as far as Spain. Later, near the end of his life, he wrote the Pastoral Epistles (1 & 2 Timothy and Titus).

The time of Paul's writings as preserved in Scripture are in four major periods:[3]

1. A.D. 51-53 (1 & 2 Thessalonians; Galatians 4): Second Journey
2. A.D. 55-57 (1 & 2 Corinthians; Romans): Third Journey
3. A.D. 60-61 (Ephesians; Colossians; Philemon; Philippians): First Roman Imprisonment[4]
4. A.D. 63-67 (1 & 2 Timothy; Titus): Second Timothy is Paul's final epistle, written during what is called the Final Roman Imprisonment. We believe Paul was beheaded by Nero in A.D. 67.

Structure

Colossians is one of the Apostle Paul's clearest, most organized epistles. It is logical in its presentation and converts easily to outline form. The reason for any outline of a biblical book is to make the book easier to understand and to make clear to modern readers the writer's flow of thought.

Paul's writings are especially easy in their basic outline because Paul's mind usually thinks of Christianity as having two strong legs upon which it stands: CHRISTIAN DOCTRINE and APPLICATION OF CHRISTIAN DOCTRINE TO LIFE. It is only our modern Christian era that attempts to divide these two great areas and even at times attempts to have these two areas oppose each other. Paul, the great systematizer of Christian doctrine and practice, always has the doctrinal (knowledge) and practical (action) intricately interwoven into a beautiful pattern that shows the magnificence of the Christian way of life. Paul does not even entertain the idea of discussing which is the most important because both reveal God's will for humankind and His desire to see Christians prosper in the way of the Lord.

Indeed, doctrine is extremely important and it forms the foundation from which our actions should flow. That is why Paul starts with doctrine first. Modern philosophy and psychology have time and time again emphasized the relationship between thinking/knowledge and action and it is so true; our thoughts and knowledge really do determine our actions. For the Apostle Paul there is always doctrine AND PAD. Paul's Doctrinal PAD is:

Doctrine AND **P**ractice

Doctrine AND **A**pplication (& **A**ction)

Doctrine AND **D**oing

Even our division of Colossians into two major sections is a man-made convenience, because the apostle's "Doctrinal PAD" frequently includes points of application in his "doctrinal" section and doctrinal points in his "practical" section. Our belief in Christ should reflect itself in its application to everyday life. Christianity is not only doctrine, it is also doing.

Below are two outlines of the Book of Colossians: a simplified outline and a more detailed outline. Anyone who wishes to really understand the flow of thought of the Book of Colossians might first read it rapidly; memorize the more detailed outline; then read it slowly at least three times, preferably in a modern translation. This will place this great book clearly in your mind and help you to locate verses and understand the mind of the apostle.

Outline
1. Introduction: Greeting, Thanksgiving, and Prayer (1:1-14)
2. The Supremacy of the Person and Work of Christ (1:15-23)
3. The Supremacy of Christ in Paul's Ministry (1:24—2:7)
4. The Supremacy of Christ Over Human Philosophy & Religious Systems (2:8-23)
5. The Supremacy of Christ in Renewed Christian Living (3:1—4:6)
6. Concluding Greetings and Commendations (4:7-18)

Analysis
1. Introduction: Greetings, Thanksgiving, and Prayer (1:1-14)
In this section Paul gives his characteristic greetings to the church at Colosse and includes his young co-worker Timothy. Paul's prayer in verses nine and ten sets the tone for the entire epistle and shows Paul's fervent prayer life and his characteristic "Doctrinal PAD." He prays in verse nine that the Colossians might have knowledge, wisdom, and spiritual understanding (KJV, and NKJ)[5] and in verse ten adds that they might "walk worthy of the Lord, fully pleasing Him, being fruitful in every good work" (NKJ). Notice that Paul sets the tone for the entire epistle by stating that the knowledge of Christ that the Colossians seek should result in their bearing fruit.

2. The Supremacy of the Person and Work of Christ (1:15-23)
In this section Paul lays the great foundation of the doctrine of Christ and establishes Him as the Being supreme to any other angelic being in heaven or any human being on earth. Christ is the Redeemer who is supreme in six areas of His person and work. Christ is:

A. The Image (Greek, *eikon*--the exact representation and manifestation) of the invisible God (v. 15).

B. The Creator of all things, both visible and invisible. The

61

KJV's terms—thrones, dominions, principalities, and powers—refer to the angelic order of invisible, but real beings that were created by Christ. The Colossians should not err and think that Christ is an angelic being; He created ALL things, including angels (v. 16).

C. Christ is the Sustainer and Uniting Principle of the entire universe (v. 17).

D. Christ is the Head of the body, the Church (v. 18).

E. Christ is the Firstborn from the dead (v. 18). His powerful resurrection from the dead establishes Him as superior to any created beings. The phrase "firstborn from the dead" establishes Him as superior even to death in that He has conquered our ultimate enemy.

F. Christ is the great Reconciler of all things. As Reconciler Christ restores the original threefold relationship between God and the creation—physical, angelic, and human. Every relationship in the universe has been affected by sin, but through Christ the original relationship is brought back from hostility to friendship.

3. The Supremacy of Christ in Paul's Ministry (1:24—2:7)

Paul has been given the privilege of preaching the mystery of Christ to the Gentiles: "Christ in you, the hope of glory" (v. 27). This phrase means, "The presence of Christ within you is the sure foundation (hope) for future resurrection and immortality (glory)."

4. The Supremacy of Christ Over Human Philosophy & Religious Systems (2:8—23)

Twice in this section Paul warns the Colossians about being cheated out of the rewards that Christians have in Christ by the philosophical and religious systems of people. In verse eight he admonishes, "Beware lest anyone cheat you through philosophy and empty deceit." In verse 18 he says, "Let no one cheat you of your reward" (NKJ). The Greek word here translated "cheat" in verse eight the NKJ and "rob" in of the KJV means to take someone as a captive. Reinecker and Rogers state that this word means "to carry off as a booty or as a captive. The word was used in the sense of 'to kidnap'...and here is the figure of carrying someone away from the truth into the slavery of error."[6] The NIV translation of verse 8 brings out clearly the force of this passage: "See to it that no one takes you captive through hollow and deceptive philosophy, which depends on human tradition and the basic principles of this world rather than on Christ." Christians can be taken into intellectual and emotional slavery through following human religious and philosophical traditions. The only way to be free is to continue to look to Christ and to stand firm and live in the way of Christ rather than live according to human philosophies.

5. The Supremacy of Christ in Renewed Christian Living (3:1—4:6)

This "practical" section covers every area of the believer's life in Christ. Just about every question regarding the Christian life has been covered by Paul in this little but powerful and thorough epistle. Paul challenges the Colossians again to get their thinking straight so that the proper actions will follow. In verse two he says, "Set your mind on things above, not on things on the earth" (NKJ). The Colossians are challenged to live according to the "new man" (NKJ, KJV) or as the NIV translates it, the "new self" (vv. 9-11). This new self will generate a new life-style of holiness and a new commitment to serve the Lord. There will be changes in: thought (3:2-4); actions (3:5-7); attitudes and speech (3:8-9); family life (3:18-21); work (3:22—4:1); and public life (4:5-6).

6. Concluding Greetings and Commendations (4:7-18)

Paul concludes with references to his many coworkers. We should never seek to serve the Lord Jesus Christ alone and in our own strength. We should work in partnership with other strong Christians who also serve the Lord with their talents and gifts. Paul mentions ten co-workers: Tychicus, Onesimus, Aristarchus, Mark, Jesus (also called Justus), Epaphras, Luke, Deman, Nymphas (male, KJV, NKJ; or Nympha-female, NIV), and Archippus. A personal study of each of these workers would yield some wonderful insights into those who assisted the apostle.

PURPOSE AND CENTRAL MESSAGE

As we study any book of the Bible we must ask two key questions: 1) Why was the book written? and 2) what central truths is the book seeking to convey? For the epistle of Colossians these questions are vital for a clear understanding of what the Lord was saying to the church at Colosse in the 1st century and what He is saying to believers today.

Purpose

Paul's letter to the Colossians was written because a serious doctrinal error had crept into the teaching and lifestyle of the church. This error lowered the person and position of Christ. A description of the problem at Colosse was reported to the apostle by Epaphras when he visited Paul during his first Roman imprisonment.

It is difficult to give a name to this error because we only know its teachings from the inferences in the Book of Colossians. From Paul's letter however, we can ascertain some of the characteristics of this false doctrine. Bible teachers refer to this teaching as the Colossian heresy.[7] Some of the elements of this erroneous religious/philosophical system are:

1. Greek Philosophical Speculation (2:8-10)
2. A Form of Jewish Legalism[8] (2:11-17)
3. A Ritualistic Religious System (2:18-23)

This religious system had some specific elements of circumcision, ceremonialism (religious observances), asceticism (practicing rigorous self-denial as a means of religious discipline and holiness), dietary regulations, and angel adoration, worship, and honor (they gave undue attention to the power of the spirits in the heavens). There also seems to have been an emphasis on some kind of special spiritual knowledge or wisdom that was considered necessary as a means of salvation. This "system" was a mixture of several diverse elements.

Many Bible scholars believe that this was an early form of a heresy that plagued the Church for its first 200 years called gnosticism (NOS-ti-sism, O as in "got," i as in "pit"). About 50 years later the Gnostics stressed the importance of knowledge (Greek, *gnosis*) for salvation. They considered the body and all matter to be evil and taught that salvation came through spiritual knowledge, not the blood of Jesus Christ. They also taught that Christ was not fully human.[9] However, no matter what name we attach to this heresy, in the final analysis this falsehood depreciated the Person and Work of Jesus Christ and Paul was compelled to write to correct this teaching.

However, the epistle is not all negative. There are other attending purposes for this letter. Paul writes to encourage the Colossians to continue in the way of the Lord and commends them for their faithfulness to the cause of Christ. Paul also sends greetings from coworkers and encourages the Colossians toward love and development of a Christian style in every area of life.

Central Message
What are the truths that the apostle and the Lord desire to communicate through this letter? In the Colossian epistle Paul wanted to communicate ONE central truth to the Colossian Church and from the central truth flows several applications.

The central message of Colossians is the supremacy, superiority, and sufficiency of Christ. Three passages from the book make this point clear:

1:18, "And He is the head of the body, the church, who is the beginning, the firstborn from the dead, that in all things He may have the preeminence" (NKJ). The NIV reads, "so that in everything he might have the supremacy."

2:3, "in whom are hidden all the treasures of wisdom and knowledge" (NKJ).

2:9-10, "For in Christ all the fullness of the Deity lives in bodily form, and you have been given fullness in Christ, who is the head over every power and authority" (NIV). The NKJ reads, "For in Him dwells all the fullness of the Godhead bodily; and you are complete in Him who is the head of all principality and power."

Supremacy means the highest in rank, authority, or quality. Paul asserts that Christ has the highest rank as Lord and Saviour of the universe and that His Person is supreme to any other in the cosmic order.

Paul states several examples to reinforce the fact of the supremacy of Christ. The supremacy of Christ is evident in that:

Christ is the Supreme Saviour in His Salvation—His redemption and reconciliation (1:12-14, 20-22). Christ is the Supreme Being in His Nature (1:15). Christ is the Supreme Creator in His Created Universe (1:16). Christ is the Supreme Head in all affairs of the Church (1:18). Christ is the Supreme Hope in concerns about our destiny (1:27). Christ is the Supreme Wisdom and Knowledge in learning (2:3). Christ is the Supreme Philosophy in matters of ethics and human theories (2:8). Christ is the Supreme Deity in bodily form (2:9). Christ is the Supreme Winner in spiritual warfare (2:15). Christ is the Supreme Sustainer in all the universe (2:17). Christ is the Supreme Life in God (3:3-4). Christ is the Supreme Forgiver in circumstances requiring kindness (3:13). Christ is the Supreme Word dwelling in us richly (3:16). Christ is the Supreme Mystery we boldly preach (4:2).

Chapters 3 and 4 can be summarized by saying: Christ is the Supreme Abiding Place in Christian living.

It is difficult to miss the point, isn't it? Jesus Christ is

Supreme over all. This is Paul's central message to both the Colossian church of the 1st century and to the 20th century church of today. There is no philosophy, religion, human system, or any other individual that can compare with the treasures of wisdom and knowledge that reside in Christ. You have the best, why even try the rest?

SCRIPTURE FOCUS

COLOSSIANS 1:1 Paul, an apostle of Jesus Christ by the will of God, and Timotheus our brother,

2 To the saints and faithful brethren in Christ which are at Colosse: Grace be unto you, and peace, from God our Father and the Lord Jesus Christ.

3 We give thanks to God and the Father of our Lord Jesus Christ, praying always for you,

4 Since we heard of your faith in Christ Jesus, and of the Love which ye have to all the saints,

12 Giving thanks unto the Father, which hath made us meet to be partakers of the inheritance of the saints in light:

13 Who hath delivered us from the power of darkness, and hath translated us into the kingdom of his dear Son:

14 In whom we have redemption through his blood, even the forgivenss of sins:

15 Who is the image of the invisible God, the firstborn of every creature:

16 For by him were all things created, that are in heaven, and that are in earth, visible and invisible, whether they be be thrones, or dominions, or principalities, or powers: all things were created by him, and for him:

17 And he is before all things, and by him all things consists.

18 And he is the head of the boy, the church: who is the beginning, the firstborn from the dead; that in all things he might have the preeminence.

19 For it pleased the Father that in him should all fulness dwell;

20 And, having made peace through the blood of his cross, by him to reconcile all things unto himself; by him, I say, whether they be things in earth, or things in heaven.

2:6 As ye have therefore received Christ Jesus the Lord, so walk ye in him:

7 Rooted and built up in him, and stablished in the faith, as ye have been taught, abounding therein with thanskgiving.

8 Beware lest any man spoil you through philosophy and vain deceit, after the tradition of men, after the rudiments of the world, and not after Christ.

9 For in him dwelleth all the fulness of the Godhead bodily.

10 And ye are complete in him, which is the head of all principality and power.

SCRIPTURE SEARCH

1. To the Colossians Paul sends _____ and _____. (1:2)
2. Paul had heard of the Colossians' _____ and _____. (1:4)
3. In Christ, we have the _____ of our _____. (1:4)
4. Jesus Christ created _____ _____ in heaven and earth. (1:16)
5. What does it mean for Christians to be "complete" in Christ? (2:10)

The African American Connection

1. The Real Saviour?

Would the REAL SAVIOUR of the Black man in America please stand up? All kinds of religious, philosophical, and political systems seem to be competing for the minds and hearts of African Americans in our "free" society. The two major political parties tell us that they each offer political salvation for Black people. One offers "family values and American traditions" and the other offers "free choice" and "equal opportunity." Certain philosophical movements offer "the power of the mind" and other religious systems offer a "religion for the Black man."

With the variety of systems and choices of religious "brands," modern day Black youth and even thinking adults may begin to wonder, Is there really a difference between Christ and the other choices? What does Christ offer that the "others" cannot or will not give? Is Christ truly the REAL SAVIOUR, or should our hope as individuals and as a race be in some "other?" The Book of Colossians was written to answer these and other questions about Christ and His supremacy over all other religions, all human systems, all spiritual forces, and all creation.

2. What do you think?

A. What is the antidote for persuasive false teachers promoting their own human wisdom in the Black community?

B. Is there really such a thing as a religion exclusively for Black Americans? Wouldn't such a "religious philosophy" be very narrow and even bigoted in its world view and outreach?

C. Why do Christians believe that Jesus Christ is THE Saviour?

D. Can one religion really be superior or supreme in relationship to another? Consider the claims, the person, the work of Christ on the Cross, His resurrection from the dead and the present–day work of the Holy Spirit. How can other religions compare?

PHILEMON:
A Letter of Love

Fred Thomas
Philemon 1-4, 8-19

Throughout the New Testament, Christians are encouraged to love each other. The Apostle John went so far as to say, "whoever does not love does not know God, because God is love" (1 John 4:8) It has been said that love can only truly be known by the action of the lover toward the beloved. Love to be love must be forgiving and it must be able to overcome sociological barriers. Paul's brief epistle, only 334 words, puts the concept of Christian love to the test. The question is, can Christian brotherly love work even in situations of severe difficulty and strain?

THE CITY OF ROME

The epistle to Philemon, written around 60 or 61 A.D., is one of the "prison epistles." These letters—Ephesians, Philippians, Colossians and Philemon—got their names because they were written by Paul, while under house arrest in Rome during his first imprisonment.

Rome was the capital of the ancient Roman Empire and later the center of Christianity. It is now the capital of modern Italy, a country located on a peninsula in southwestern Europe. The city itself is located in west central Italy about 15 miles from the mouth of the Tiber River.[1]

According to tradition, the Roman Empire was founded on April 27, 753 B. C. It was named after its founder, Romulas, who ruled 37 years before mysteriously disappearing, supposedly taken up to heaven. The empire was only a narrow strip along

71

the Mediterranean Sea until 338 B.C. when it took control of central Italy. Then came the Punic Wars (264-146 B.C.), a series of wars between Rome and Carthage, a city located in North Africa.

During the second Punic War (218-202 B.C.), Hannibal, the great African general, crossed the Alps with a herd of elephants and defeated two large Roman armies striking, fear in the Roman populace. Hannibal was finally defeated in 202 and Carthage became a Roman tributary until it was finally destroyed in 147 B.C. Palestine was conquered in 63 B.C. Julius Caesar consolidated the vast empire between 58 and 51 B.C.[2]

THE CHURCH IN ROME

There is some controversy over who started the church in Rome. Roman Catholic tradition claims the Apostle Peter founded the church, but this is challenged by the following considerations:

In the last chapter of the Book of Romans, Paul salutes 27 men by name but doesn't mention Peter. Had Peter been there, Paul surely would have saluted him. Secondly, Paul stated that it had always been his ambition to preach the Gospel where it had not been heard, "So that I would not be building on someone else's foundation" (Romans 15:20), but he wanted to go to Rome.

Thirdly, Luke was a careful historian yet, in the Book of Acts he did not record Peter as the founder of the church. If an apostle as prominent as Peter had founded the church in Rome, surely Luke would have said so.[3]

Another theory is the church was founded by converts from churches in Asia established by Paul. The best candidates for this theory are Aquila and Priscilla, whom we first meet in Ephesus in the 18th chapter of Acts. Rufus, the son of Simon the Cyrenian, the Black man who carried the cross of Jesus (Matthew 15:21), is also mentioned as a possible founder. All are referred to in the salutation of Romans 11. Most probable is that the church was founded by Jews and proselytes, present in Jerusalem on the Day of Pentecost, who then returned home to Rome. The church was tolerated in Rome because Romans were polytheists, persons who believe in and worship many gods. Polytheism by its indefinite nature cannot presume to have a complete knowledge of God. At first Christians were not distinguished from Jews but shared in the acceptance that was given to Judaism as the national religion of a Roman territory.[4] The Church was well known throughout the empire (Romans 1:8). The Christian population was large and met in several different houses (Romans 16). Tacitus, a noted historian, described the Christian population of Rome as an "immense multitude."

God used both nations and individuals to prepare the way for the Gospel. Of all the nations God used, Rome was one of the most important. Rome paved the way for the Gospel by building roads throughout the vast empire, making travel easier and thereby facilitating the spread of the Good News. The Pax Romana or Roman Law policed the roads, protecting the missionaries from violence. It was a Roman governor who condemned Christ to crucifixion. Both Peter and Paul were martyred in Rome. Titus, a Roman general, destroyed Jerusalem in 70 A.D. In 313 A.D. under Constantine, Christianity became the state religion of Rome.

THE LETTER

Structure
1. Intercession (Philemon 1:1-16)
   A. Greetings (1:1-3)
   B. Prayer for Philemon (1:4-6)
   C. Plea for Onesimus (1:7-16)

2. Imputation
   A. Paul Identifies with Onesimus (1:17)
   B. Paul Assumes Onesimus's Debt (1:18-9)
   C. Paul Expresses Confidence in Philemon (1:20-22)
   D. Conclusion (1:23-25)

Analysis

The letter to Philemon is one of four epistles addressed to individuals. The other three are: 1st and 2nd Timothy and Titus. It is unique, noteworthy, and very significant to the Gospel message. The Philemon epistle is unique because it is the only epistle addressed to a personal friend, regarding a personal matter. It is noteworthy because it addresses the issue of slavery. (Onesimus was a runaway slave who belonged to Paul's friend Philemon.) It is significant because it demonstrates the power of the Gospel to save (Romans 1:16). Philemon, Onesimus, Apphia, and Archippus, all mentioned by name in the address, were all converted to Christianity as a result of Paul proclaiming the Gospel.

But the letter's most important contribution to the kingdom of God is its picture of Christ in His role as intercessor: "I appeal to you for my son Onesimus" (v. 10), and as substitute: "If he has done you any wrong...charge it to me" (v. 18).

In this beautiful epistle Paul reveals himself as a man of humor, humility, tact, and love. He reveals the Church as a place where all barriers between people are broken down: "Here there is not Greek or Jew, circumcised or uncircumcised, Barbarian, Scythian, slave or free, but Christ is all, and in all" (Colossians 3:11).

1. Intercession (Philemon 1:1-16)

A. *Greetings (1:1-3).* Paul immediately identifies himself with Onesimus. He drops his usual title of apostle and calls himself a prisoner. Who better to plead the cause of one in bondage than someone else in bondage? Like Jesus who clothed Himself in flesh to plead the cause of flesh (John 1:14; 17:1-25), the Apostle Paul stresses his bondage to intercede for a slave.

In Philemon 1:2 the apostle reveals a bit of Pauline humor. He indulges himself in some fine word play of people's names he is addressing. Philemon, whose name means friendly or affectionate, is called "dear friend." Archippus, meaning master of the horse, is called "fellow soldier." Great soldiers and warriors of ancient times were known for their horsemanship. Paul will return to this pun later when discussing Onesimus.[5]

Although the letter is addressed primarily to Philemon, it is to be shared with others. Apphia, probably Philemon's wife, likely was one of them. The term "our sister" demonstrates that she was also a baptized member of the Church. Paul, addressing her in the greeting, hints at the elevated status of women under Christianity. Archippus, another probable part of Paul's audience, was either Philemon's son or a family friend. There is strong evidence that Archippus was the minister of the church meeting in Philemon's house.[6]

During the first two centuries of Christianity, the Church did not build temples or special buildings to hold services. All their resources went into spreading the Good News, and they met in the homes of some of the wealthier converts. The story of John Martyr, executed by Romans in the third century, beautifully illustrates the feeling of the Church at that time.

"When on trial, before the Roman prefect, the prefect said to John Martyr, 'Where do you Christians assemble?' John Martyr said, 'We do not as you suppose, meet in one place; for our God, the God of Christians fills the heaven and the earth, and therefore He is present anywhere. We can meet anyplace and have communion and fellowship with Him. When I go to Rome, I have a home where I can go and remain; and those Christians who desire to hear me teach come into that home.'"[7]

In Phileman 1:3, Paul combines the Hebrew peace *(shalom)* with the Greek grace *(charis)* into one greeting, demonstrating that Christ transcends and at the same time unites the races of man.[8]

B. Prayer for Philemon (1:4-6). The mingling of thanksgiving and intercession is true prayer. God as the source of all good is due all gratefulness. Paul begins by thanking God for Philemon's faith in Christ as the sole source of salvation, the sender of the Holy Spirit, and the only access to God's blessing. Then he expresses his gratitude for Philemon's love for all the saints.

Love is the action by which Philemon demonstrates his faith. Love is an act of the human will, not the result of human emotion. It is impartial, non-discriminating, and active. It seeks the good of others while expecting nothing in return, because it is based on faith in Christ as the supplier of all one's needs.

By stressing Philemon's love for ALL the saints, Paul is leading up to his plea for Onesimus who is now one of the saints. The apostle tactfully sets the stage for his intercession by praying that Philemon would be "active in sharing his faith" (v. 6) as a means of increasing his own knowledge of God. Paul knew that if Philemon would exercise forgiveness by faith, he would acquire a more in-depth knowledge of God's forgiveness. A. Maclarin stated, "If a man does not live up to his religion, his religion shrinks to the level of his life."[9] The practice of convictions deepens convictions. It is the cup that is emptied that will be filled to overflowing.

C. Plea for Onesimus (1:7-16). The apostle now begins to intercede directly for Onesimus. He bases his plea on five points:

(1) PHILEMON'S REPUTATION (vv. 5 and 7). Word of Philemon's acts of kindness had traveled across the continent and even reached Paul in Rome. Paul was requesting that the same love which had refreshed the hearts of so many others now be expressed toward his own slave.

(2) CHRISTIAN LOVE (vv. 8-9). Although Paul had every right as an apostle to order Philemon to forgive Onesimus, he chose to appeal to Philemon's love. He wanted Philemon to demonstrate love willingly, not grudgingly demonstrate obedience. He based his loving request on his own bondage for the cause of Christ, and his age, about 60 at the time. Although 60 was and is a good age, Paul's many labors, trials and perils had probably caused him to age prematurely. According to 2 Corinthians 11:16, he had received 39 lashes five times; three times he had been beaten with rods. He was stoned once. He experienced three different shipwrecks, once spending an entire day and night on the open sea. In his various travels he was often in danger from rivers, bandits, his own countrymen, Gentiles and false brothers. He had gone without food and sleep, and he had been cold and naked. All this on top of the daily pressures of worrying about all the new churches he had established. How could Philemon, his "beloved friend" refuse this old imprisoned warrior's request?

(3) ONESIMUS' CONVERSION (v. 10). Paul calls Onesimus his son. Philemon would have to respect anyone Paul called by so tender a name, for he too was a spiritual son of the apostle. Onesimus would never again be simply a slave, he was now Philemon's Christian brother. This did not mean that Onesimus was no longer a slave or that he was not to be judged for running away and possibly stealing. But it did mean that his new standing had to be considered when judging his case.

(4) ONESIMUS'S VALUE TO PAUL (vv. 11-14). Paul returns to the pun he started in verses one and two. Onesimus means profitable,[10] and Paul uses a play on words, saying that Onesimus had not been very profitable to Paul in the past, but had become very useful to both Paul and Philemon. So valuable in fact that Paul had wanted to keep Onesimus with him but sent him back. The verb translated "sending him" in verse 12 also means to "refer a case to." In effect Paul is saying to Philemon, "I am referring the case of Onesimus, who is my very heart, to

you." Then he begins his appeal: "I would have liked to have kept him with me" (v. 13).

Onesimus had become so useful to the ministry in Rome and such a comfort to Paul that he wanted to keep him, but would do nothing without Philemon's consent (v. 14). All Christian decisions must be based on free will submitted to love. True Christianity is always voluntary service, not forced obedience.

(5) THE PROVIDENCE OF GOD (vv. 15-16). "And we know that in all things God works for the good of those who love him..." (Romans 8:28, NIV). Paul is not dogmatic here, but he suggests the possibility that this entire situation is an act of divine will. Just as in the story of Joseph (Genesis 50:20), what Onesimus intended for harm, God intended for good to accomplish what was now being done. A temporal relationship had become eternal, he that had been unprofitable was now profitable. A slave had not been lost, but a dear brother had been gained.[11]

Paul has tactfully and tenderly convinced his friend that he should forgive and receive Onesimus back. But the problem is that if Philemon overlooks the crimes of Onesimus, it may encourage other slaves to convert to Christianity as a means of gaining influence with their masters. A crime had been committed, and justice demanded that someone pay the penalty.

2. Imputation (1:17-25)

A. *Paul Identifies with Onesimus (1:17).* There is no way that Onesimus could approach Philemon with any merit of his own, he was guilty and worthy of punishment. This is an illustration of what Christ has done for all believers. Christians are so identified with Christ that God receives them as He receives His Son. This is what Paul asked of Philemon, "welcome him as you would welcome me." The word welcome is from a Greek word meaning to welcome into one's family circle. Just as Christians who are identified with Christ are welcomed into the family of

78

God, Paul asked Philemon to accept Onesimus as a Christian brother and welcome him into his family—the same as if it were Paul himself.

B. Paul assumes Onesimus's Debt (1:18-19). Onesimus might have stolen from Philemon when he ran away. If so, his offense included monetary loss as well as the losses incurred by the slave's running away. Just as God in His holiness could not ignore the debt that Christians owe and remain faithful to His own law, Philemon could not simply ignore the crimes of Onesimus. Paul offered the perfect solution: "charge it to me" (v. 18). This is called imputation, to charge to one's account what doesn't belong to him or her. This request by Paul beautifully illustrates the sinless Saviour taking on the sins of the world: "God made him who had no sin to be sin for us, so that in him we might become the righteousness of God" (1 Corinthians 5:21). It is Christ's own example that Paul is attempting to follow here. He offers a covenant signed with his own hand (Philemon 1:19) as the basis for the new relationship Philemon and Onesimus could now enjoy.

There is an inference here that Paul led Philemon to Christ. If so, Philemon and Onesimus were now spiritual brothers; they shared the same spiritual Father.

C. Paul Expresses Confidence in Philemon (1:20-22). Considering the new relationship between Paul, Philemon, and Onesimus, how could Philemon not forgive Onesimus? But there is the hint here that forgiveness and restoration were not all Paul had in mind. Was he hinting at freedom? William Alexander suggest, "Yet there was a very general feeling that the word liberty fills St. Paul's heart and hovers over his pen though unwritten."[12] To speak out against slavery would have meant the condemnation of Christianity in every city throughout the empire. But what could not be done publicly could be hinted at subtly, not changing governments, but changing people one heart at a time.

D. Conclusion (1:23-25). Paul closes the letter by acknowledging those present with him and giving a benediction. Before he launches into the salutation he takes care of one last piece of outstanding business. The apostle does not request prayer, but he takes it for granted that the saints are praying for his release. He fully expects their prayers to be answered and requests that Philemon prepare a room for him to stay. He closes the letter by praying that grace of God would be Philemon's spirit. It is significant that Paul, who asked Philemon to extend loving grace to a guilty slave, would close by praying that God's grace would be present with Philemon.

PURPOSE AND CENTRAL MESSAGE

Philemon was a wealthy slave owner who was a member of the church in Colosse. Onesimus, his slave, had run away and somehow ended up in Rome where he met the Apostle Paul. Paul had led him to Christ (v. 10) and he had become a valued asset to the ministry in Rome as well as a comfort to Paul himself. Then something happened; maybe Onesimus in a fit of conscience confessed his situation to Paul. Or maybe it was the appearance of Epaphras, the leader of the Colossian church in Rome that brought the matter to Paul's attention. Whatever the reason Onesimus had to return to Philemon. Paul had grown to love Onesimus (v. 12) and wanted to keep Onesimus with him (v. 13), but it would be wrong to do so without Philemon's consent (v. 14).[13]

Purpose

Paul wrote this brief epistle as his personal appeal to Philemon for grace and mercy in the case of Onesimus. His position was particularly difficult because he was spiritual father to both parties. S. Davidson called this letter the "polite epistle" because of its diplomacy, charm, and grace.[14]

The returning of Onesimus to Philemon was not without risk. First of all was the danger of slave catchers. To overcome this

Paul sent Tychicus along with Onesimus to Colosse (v. 12). But the greater danger awaited Onesimus after his arrival in Colosse. Under Roman law a slave had no rights. He was the personal property of his master and subject to his whims. William Barclay relates the story of Vedius Pollio and how he treated one of his slaves: "The slave was carrying a tray of crystal goblets into the courtyard; he dropped and broke one, on the instant Pollio ordered him thrown into the fishpond in the middle of the court, where savage lampreys tore him to pieces."[15]

The punishment for runaway slaves might be a flogging or imprisonment. He could possibly be branded in the forehead with a red hot iron. In some case the slave could be tortured to death.[16]

In the antebellum South the Bible was used to justify slavery. One of the arguments was, "If slavery is so wrong, why did Jesus and the apostles say nothing against it?" In the epistles to the churches in Colosse and Ephesus, Paul gave instructions regulating slavery, but nowhere was it condemned. The letter to Philemon was the perfect opportunity for Paul to speak out against slavery and order Philemon to set Onesimus free. According to Lightfoot, "The word emancipation seems to tremble on his lips, but he never utters it.[17]

For the infant church to attack slavery would have been disastrous. Slavery was essential to the ancient world. Estimates suggest that there were as many as 60 million slaves in the Roman Empire ranging in price from $80 for a common laborer to about $8,000 for a skilled slave. Like the American South, the economies of the ancient world were built on the backs of forced labor.[18] If the young church had openly spoken out against slavery it would have been crushed, and the message of the Gospel would have become confused with calls for social change.

The purpose of the Gospel has never been to change nations and empires, but people. It tears down barriers between people. In Christ there is neither Greek nor Jew, circumcision

81

nor uncircumcision, Barbarian, Scythian, slave or free..."
(Colossians 3:11). The church could not speak out openly
against slavery, but it could and did introduce a new relationship
between slave and master. A relationship based on the brotherhood of man under the Fatherhood of God. The Bible did in fact
speak out against slavery but the message was subtle. What kind
of man would inflict the cruelty of slavery upon his brother,
when in the body of Christ all men are brothers? Paul was so
sure Philemon would understand this that after asking that
Onesimus be forgiven and welcomed back, he wrote he was sure
that Philemon would do even more than he asked. What more
could Philemon do other than granting Onesimus his complete
freedom?

Central Message

The central message of this small but powerful book is the
brotherhood of man under the Fatherhood of God. Believers are
baptized into the body of Christ where all divisions cease to
exist. In Christ there is neither Jew nor Greek, circumcision nor
uncircumcision, Barbarian, Scythian, slave nor free: but Christ is
all and in all (Colossians 3:11). Social institutions such as race,
culture, and status are torn down in the body of Christ. God is
the Father of all, and all are brothers and sisters.

Another important theme is the emphasis on the virtues of
grace and mercy. The slave Onesimus had committed an injustice against his owner Philemon and he deserved to be punished.
Paul's plea was for Philemon to forego all punishment. This is
the best definition of mercy, not giving persons what they justly
deserve. Instead Paul requested that Onesimus be welcomed
back. What had Onesimus done to deserve such a welcome?
Nothing at all. This is grace, undeserved favor, giving persons
what they do not deserve and cannot earn.

Finally, this very personal epistle demonstrates the
doctrines of identification and imputation. We are all identified with Onesimus, guilty of not just running away from

our Master, but compounding our alienation by sin. Onesimus could not approach Philemon on his own merit, so Paul said to welcome Onesimus as if he were Paul. We cannot approach God based on our merit, but because we are identified with Christ we can boldly enter into the presence of the Most High and charge to Christ's account what does not belong to Him. When considering Onesimus's crime Paul said, "Charge it to my account...I will repay." When Jesus hung on the cross and uttered the words, "It is finished," He paid in full the cost of reconciling us to God. Because of sin we deserve death, but Christ died once and for all and freed us from the power of death.

SCRIPTURE FOCUS

PHILEMON 1 Paul, a prisoner of Jesus Christ, and Timothy our brother, unto Philemon our dearly beloved, and fellow labourer,

2 And to our beloved Apphia and Archippus our fellow soldier, and to the church in thy house:

3 Grace to you, and peace, from God our Father and the Lord Jesus Christ.

4 I thank my God, making mention of thee always in my prayers,

8 Wherefore, though I might be much bold in Christ to enjoin thee that which is convenient,

9 Yet for love's sake I rather beseech thee, being such an one as Paul the aged, and now also a prisoner of Jesus Christ.

10 I beseech thee for my son Onesimus, whom I have begotten in my bonds:

11 Which in time past was to thee unprofitable, but now profitable to thee and to me:

12 *Whom I have sent again: thou therefore receive him, that is, mine own bowels:*

13 *Whom I would have retained with me, that in thy stead he might have ministered unto me in the bonds of the gospel:*

14 *But without thy mind would I do nothing; that thy benefit should not be as it were of necessity, but willingly.*

15 *For perhaps he therefore departed for a season, that thou shouldest receive him for ever;*

16 *Not now as a servant, but above a servant, a brother beloved, specially to me, but how much more unto thee, both in the flesh, and in the Lord?*

17 *If thou count me therefore a partner, receive him as myself.*

18 *If he hath wronged thee, or oweth thee ought, put that on mine account;*

19 *I Paul have written it with mine own hand, I will repay it: albeit I do not say to thee how thou owest unto me even thine own self besides.*

SCRIPTURE SEARCH

This letter is written by _____ (v. 1) to _____ (v. 1) on behalf of _____ (v. 10) who had been a slave, but was now a _____ in Christ.

The African American Connection

The Chattel racial slavery that occurred in America was the worst form of slavery in the history of humankind. Physical bondage was probably the least harmful aspect of this slavery. The conscience effort on the part of slave owners to dehumanize and snatch away the history and heritage of the enslaved people had far reaching effects and, in some cases, are now only being overcome.

Although the Emancipation Proclamation legally ended the practice of slavery in the United States, various insidious forms of slavery continue to plague African American people. Alcohol and drug addiction are new forms of physical bondage. The break down in the family structure and the idea that Black people are somehow dependent on the government to address the problems in our communities are subtle forms of mental bondage.

To completely throw off the yoke of bondage, we as a people must return to the same techniques that our ancestors used to survive years of slavery and segregation. First of all, we must depend on Christ as the ultimate source of our strength. Secondly, strong family units must be nurtured and taught to our young people. Finally, we must reestablish a sense of community built on respect for the elderly and anchored by the church. True freedom is not the absence of chains, but the presence of spiritual, emotional, and mental liberty. "Whom the Lord sets free is free indeed" (John 8:36, paraphrased).

FOOTNOTES

GALATIANS

1. Charles Layman, *The Interpretor's One-Volume Commentary On The Bible.* (Nashville: Abingdon Press, 1971) p. 824

2. Albert Barnes, *Barnes Notes on The New Testament.* (Grand Rapids: Kregel Publishers, 1962) p. 913

3. William Barclay, *The Letters of Galatians and Ephesians.* (Philedelphia: Westminster Press, 1976)

4. Layman, p. 824

5. Barnes, p. 919

6. Barclay, p. 10

7. J.B. Lyles, *The Preacher's Outline and Sermon Bible.* (LaGrange, GA, 1989) p. 16

8. *Ibid.,* p. 89

9. *Ibid.,* p. 89

10. *Ibid.,* p. 89

EPHESIANS

1. Irving Jensen, *Jensen's Survey of The New Testament.* (Chicago: Moody Press, 1981) p. 314.

2. Samuel Kepler, *Interpreter's Dictionary of the Bible.* (Nashville: Abingdon Press, 1989) p. 154.

3. F.L. Cross and E.A. Livingstone, *Oxford Dictionary of the Christian Church.* (London: Oxford University Press, 1974) p. 461.

4. *Universal Edition of the New Standard Encylopedia.* (Chicago: Standard Educational Corporation, 1977) p. 189.

5. Merrill Unger, *Bible Handbook.* (Chicago: Moody Press, 1970) p. 671.

6. Leslie Mitton, *The New Century Bible Commentary: Ephesians.* (Grand Rapids: Eerdmans, 1973). p. 40.

7. Jensen, p. 315.

8. Unger, p. 678.

9. Mitton, p. 210.

10. Kepler, p. 854

11. Raymond Brown, *Jerome Bible Commentary.* (Englewood Cliffs, NJ:

Prentice Hall, 1990) p. 890

12. Nolan Harmon, Editor. *The Interpreter's Bible X.* (Nashville: Abingdon Press, 1981) p. 844.

PHILIPPIANS

1. Kahlil Gibran, *the Prophet* (New York: Knopf, 1983 edition) Martin Luther King, Jr. *Strength to Love* (New York, Harber 1963). Howard Thurman: *Disciplines of The Spirit* (Richmond, Indiana, Friends United Press, 1987 edition).

2. See Acts 15:40, 16:1-4,11.

3. Unger, Merrill, *Archaeology and The New Testament* (Grand Rapids: Academic Books, 1962) p. 216

4. Unger, p. 216, see also Sir William Ramsey. *St. Paul the Traveller and Roman Citizen*

5. Charles Pfeiffer and Howard Vos, *The Wycliff Historical Geography of Bible Lands.* (Chicago: Moody Press, 1967) p. 451

6. Unger, P. 219 See also Gromacki, *New Testament Survey.* (Grand Rapids: Baker, 1974) p. 256

7. Gromacki, p. 256

8. Unger, p. 216

9. The story of the founding of the Philippian church is found in Acts 15:40—16:40.

COLOSSIANS

1. William Hendricksen, *Exposition of Colossians and Philemon.* (Grand Rapids: Baker Book House, 1964), p. 10.

2. *Ibid.,* p. 15.

3. There is some variation regarding specific dates in the life of the Apostle Paul. However, the dates given here would be generally accepted. (See *New International Version, 1985; pp. 1664-1665)*

4. There is some debate among New Testament scholars as to the exact time of the writing of Galatians. The minority view is that it was written A.D. 48 or 49 on Paul's first journey. The view given in this study (A.D. 51-53, second journey) is generally accepted as accurate.

5. Three Bible translations will be used in this study: the *New International Version* will be called NIV; the *New King James Version* will be called NKJV; the *King James Version* will be called KJV.

6. Fritz Rienecker and Cleon Rogers, *Linquistic Key to the Greek New Testament.* (Grand Rapids: Zondervan, 1980), p. 573.

7. Heresy (Her-ees-see) is a term that has somewhat come to disuse in the Church today, but it refers to opinions and doctrines that are contrary to the accepted teachings and truths of the Christian Church, particularly in relationship to the doctrines of God, Christ and salvation.

8. Legalism in a religious sense means strict adherence to any law or set of rules. These rules are considered by legalists as also necessary for salvation. As a result they usually detract from the power of Christ's death and resurrection alone to save. The forms of Jewish legalism in the time of the Apostle Paul and the various forms of Christian legalism in modern times say, "Yes, Christ is necessary for salvation, but so also are our rules."

9. If you wish to further investigate gnosticism see the article in *The International Standard Bible Encyclopedia,* 1982. This fully revised edition of *ISBE* in four volumes has excellent articles on most any bible topic. The one on gnosticism is recommended only for those with a deeper interest in this philosophy.

PHILEMON

1. William Smith, *Smith's Bible Dictionary.* (McLean, VA: McDonald Publishing) p. 263

2. H.L. Wilmington, *Wilmington's Guide to The Bible.* (Wheaton, IL: Tyndale House, 1981) p. 939

3. Alva McClain, *Romans: The Gospel of God's Grace.* (Chicago: Moody Press, 1973) pp. 13-14.

4. James Orr, et al. *The International Standard Bible Encylopedia IV.* (Grand Rapids: Eerdmans, 1939) pp. 2613-2618

5. Jerome Smith, *The New Treasury of Scripture Knowledge.* (Nashville: Nelson Publishers, 1992) p. 1441

6. Joseph Excell, *The Bible Illustrator.* (Grand Rapids: Baker, 1973) p. 19

7. McClain, p. 248.

8. W.E. Vines, *Expository Dictionary of New Testament Words.* (Chicago: Moody Press, 1940) pp. 169-170

9. Excell, p. 35

10. Smith, p. 1441

11. Warren Wiersbe, *The Bible Exposition Commentary II.* (Wheaton IL.: Victor Books, 1989) p. 271

12. Excell, p. 82

13. William Barclay, *The Letters to Timothy, Titus, and Philemon.* (Philadelphia: Westminster Press, 1975) p. 270

14. S. Davidson, in Excell, p. 6

15. Barclay, p. 270

16. Excell, p. 6

17. Barclay, p. 271

18. Wiersbe, p. 270

BIBLIOGRAPHY

Barclay, William. *Letters to Galatians and Ephesians.* Philadelphia: Westminster Press, 1976.

Barclay, William. *Letters To Philippians, Colossians and Thessalonians.* Philadelphia: Westminster Press, 1975.

Barclay, William. *Letters To Timothy, Titus and Philemon.* Philadelphia: Westminster Press, 1975.

Barnes, Albert. *Barnes' Notes on the New Testament.* Grand Rapids: Kregel, 1963.

Brown, Raymond. *The New Jerome Biblical Commentary.* Englewood Cliffs, New Jersey: Prentice Hall, 1990.

Bryant, T. Alton. *The New Compact Bible Dictionary.* Grand Rapids: Zondervan, 1967.

Buttick, George. *The Interpreter's Dictionary of The Bible.* Nashville: Abingdon Press, 1989.

Duncan, G.S. "Letter to the Philippians," *The Interpreter's Dictionary of the Bible, Vol. 3,* edited by George A. Buttrick. Nashville: Abingdon Press, 1982 edition.

Dunnett, Walter M. *New Testament Survey.* Wheaton: Evangelical Teacher Training Association, 1983.

Earle, Ralph. *Word Meanings in the N.T.* Grand Rapids: Baker Book House, 1988.

Elwell, Walter A. *Baker's Bible Handbook.* Grand Rapids: Baker Book House 1989.

Gromacki, Robert. *New Testament Survey.* Grand Rapids: Baker Book House, 1974.

Harmon, Nolan. *The Interpreter's Bible.* Nashville: Abingdon Press, 1981.

Irwin, C.H. *The Everyday Bible Commentary.* Grand Rapids: Zondervan, 1928.

Jensen, Irving L. *Philippians.* Chicago: Moody Press, 1973.

Jensen, Irving L. *Jensen's Survey of the New Testament.* Chicago: Moody Press, 1981.

Landis, Besson. *An Outline of the Bible Book by Book.* New York: Barnes & Noble Books, 1963.

Langer, William. *An Encyclopedia of World History.* Boston: Houghton Mifflin, 1940.

Lawson, LeRoy. *God's Word A.D.* Cincinnati: New Life Books, 1983.

Layman, Charles M. *The Interpreter's Commentary on The Bible.* Nashville: Abingdon Press, 1980.

Layman, Charles M. *The Interpreter's Commentary, Volume One.* Nashville: Abingdon Press, 1971.

Le Peace, Andrew and Phyllis. *Ephesians.* Downers Grove, Il: InterVarsity Press, 1985.

Lockyer, Herbert. *All The Men of the Bible.* Grand Rapids: Zondervan, 1958.

Longenecker, Richard N. *The Ministry and Message of Paul.* Grand Rapids: Zondervan, 1971.

McClain, Alva J. *Romans: The Gospel of God's Grace.* Chicago: Moody Press, 1973.

Meyer, E.B. *Bible Commentary.* Wheaton, Il.: Tyndale, 1979

Mitton, Leslie C. *The New Century Bible Commentary: Ephesians.* Grand Rapids: Eerdmans, 1973.

Muller, Jac J. *The Epistles of Paul to the Philippians and to Philemon.* Grand Rapids: Eerdmans, 1976.

Neil, William. *The New Century Bible Commentary: The Acts of the Apostle.* Grand Rapids: Eerdmans, 1973.

Orr, James. *The International Standard Bible Encyclopedia.* Grand Rapids: Eerdmans, 1939.

Ramsay, William M. *The Layman's Guide to the New Testament.* Atlanta: John Knox Press, 1981.

Smith, Jerome H. *The New Treasury of Scripture Knowledge.* Nashville: Nelson Publishers, 1992.

Smith, William D. *Smith's Bible Dictionary.* McClean, VA: McDonald Publishing.

Unger, Merrill F. *Bible Handbook.* Chicago: Moody Press, 1970.

Vines, W. E. *A Dictionary of New Testament Words.* Chicago: Moody Press, 1940.

Walvoord, John. *Philippians: Triumph in Christ* Chicago: Moody Press, 1971.

Wiersbe, Warren W. *Be Rich.* Wheaton, IL: Victor Books, 1976.

Wiersbe, Warren. *The Bible Exposition Commentary, 2 Vols.* Wheaton, IL: Victor Books, 1989.

Williams, Charles. *A Commentary On The Pauline Epistles.* Chicago: Moody Press, 1953.

Wilmington, H. L. *Wilmington's Guide To the Bible.* Wheaton, IL: Tyndale, 1981.

Wuest, Kenneth. *Philippians In The Greek New Testament for The English Reader.* Grand Rapids: Eerdmans, 1942.

BIBLES

Caldwell, Ryrie C. *The Ryrie Study Bible, New Testament.* Chicago: Moody Press, 1976.

Harmon, Nolan B. *The Interpreter's Bible, Volume 10.* Nashville: Abingdon Press, 1981.

The Interpreter's Dictionary of the Bible. Nashville: Abingdon Press, 1989.

(KJV) *The King James Version*

(NIV) *The New International Version*

(JB) *The New Jerome Bible Commentary*

(OAB) *The New Oxford Annotated Bible*

BIOGRAPHIES

Mary Carr, M.Div., Pastor at Christian Heritage Training Center Community Church, Chicago, Illinois.

Bennie Goodwin, Ph.D., Senior Editor at Urban Ministries, Inc., Chicago, Illinois.

Marvin Goodwin, M.A., Professor of History at Kennedy-King College, Chicago, Illinois.

Kenneth Hammonds, Ed.D., Director of Christian Education, West Angeles Church of God in Christ, Los Angeles, California.

Fred Thomas, B.A., Assistant to the President at Urban Ministries, Inc., Chicago, Illinois.

ALSO AVAILABLE FROM UMI

In Step With the Master
Upon This Rock
Falling Love With God
Seeing With the Heart
Africans Who Shaped Our Faith
How I Got Over
Biblical Strategies for a Community in Crisis
How to Equip the African American Family
How to Help Hurting People
How to Pray & Communicate with God
Ordinary People Can Do the Extraordinary

Leader Guides are also available for teaching these subjects in mid-week Bible study, adult and young adult Sunday School, Church retreats and training hour.